Marilyn,

You are missed! Thanks for all the laughs. Each day is a gift!

[signature]

Five Days With Dad

PATRICK MCSHANE

Five Days With Dad
©2022, Patrick McShane

All rights reserved. This book or any portion thereof may not be reproduced or used in any manner whatsoever without the express written permission of the publisher except for the use of brief quotations in a book review.

ISBN: 978-1-66787-556-9
ISBN eBook: 978-1-66787-557-6

To Theresa, Jillian, Kathleen and Caroline.
Thank you for reminding me to chase my dreams.

Preface

My blue Infinity zipped down a side road going a little faster than what the posted speed limit suggested (okay, demanded). Trees whipped past as a random DJ talked about how he cannot function without his morning coffee while his team of sycophants laughed hysterically.

The bend in the road caused all passengers bodies to sway a bit... the product of advanced speed and a distracted driver. No passenger made mention of the momentary jolt. The car is much like its driver, getting on a bit in years and thinks of itself as a sport model but is very much simply a reliable sedan. My wife, Theresa, comfortably sat in the passenger side and our three daughters, Jillian, Kathleen and Caroline were tightly packed in the back.

My mind drifted from where I was heading to thinking of the days I'm missing at work and my mounting responsibilities. What an asshole. Seriously, why are these thoughts in my head? Does every moment have to be about me? The owner of the business told me to take as much time as I needed. Truth be told, I was not that instrumental to that businesses' success.

I accelerated through Natick center, slowing only for a series of cross walks put in every 50 yards that normally culminated with a police cruiser that gently nestled itself in about a block down the street from Middlesex Savings. Did I close the garage door. Who cares? I would feel bad for the person who broke in to rob my house. Kind of futile effort. We are preparing to put three kids through college, not a whole lot of luxuries cluttering up the place. The DJ is now wondering who are all these people on the road when he drives in to the station at 5 AM.. His team howls with laughter. Does anyone not on his payroll find any of this amusing?

My breathing is now coming in elongated gasps - I didn't really notice until Theresa gently pointed it out. "You okay?" She asked. The kids remained silent. "Yeah, I'm fine," I say as I slightly shake my head no. My head was telling the truth, my words were damn liars.

One of the kids has a doctor's appointment sometime this week. I don't know which one. I don't have any idea who their doctor is let alone if I have any responsibility with getting them to or from this appointment. All I know is that this appointment is now living in a part of my brain that should have another tenant.

I cringed as I took a looping right onto Route 30 in Wayland. I meant to drop suits at the dry cleaner earlier this week. For some reason, God wanted me to remember at this moment that they are lying, crumpled in the far corner of my bedroom, tucked in next to my bureau, partially hidden by a large wicker hamper that has a lid with a broken handle.

"Get out of my head," I repeated to myself. Why would such mundane, stupid information be blocking out what I assume I should be thinking about. Everyone in the car was eerily silent. I had already seen my father alive for the last time. Today I was going to see him dead for the last time. We were now about fifteen minutes from Joyce Funeral Home in Waltham, Massachusetts. Following a brief gathering there, we would head down the street to Saint Charles Church.

As I drove, I willed myself to focus more on the moments spent with my parents. After they retired to Florida I would only have an opportunity to see them once or twice a year. Each visit was remarkably unremarkable. We would sit in their dining or living room, and eat something that moments ago was separated from the frying pan with a large, heavy metallic spatula. We would discuss the never-ending changes in my life (when kids are younger there is always some drama unfolding, or a new dream being chased). Mostly, though, I listened to their stories of a lifetime. All the stories shaped them, and directly impacted how they raised me and my siblings.

As I came over a small hill in Waltham, I could see Joyce Funeral Home up the road on the left hand side. The police were already directing traffic to allow for an easy entrance. I was the fourth car in the parking lot that morning. We got out and began walking across to the heavy wooden doors where a man stood. His gray hair was neatly combed and his charcoal suit was pristine. He gave a respectful nod as he opened the door allowing my family entrance. I wondered if he needed to get his suit cleaned and pressed after each wear to get it to look that crisp.

Immediately inside, we stopped and glanced at the frames containing the collection of pictures that were gathered to show wonderful memories of my father's life. With each picture a story would coming flooding back into my brain. I had heard them so many times I could recite them verbatim. I knew how much I would miss hearing his voice tell these stories. Before he passed I had vowed to store away his stories, voice, dialect, mannerisms and facial expressions in my head.

The one thing I knew, I had the stories…and not just in my head. Over the last few years, following each visit to their home in Clearwater, Florida, I would jot pages and pages of notes onto a collection of yellow legal pads. When I returned home I dropped these notes in a W.B. Mason computer paper box that was kept on a shelf in my closet. It was my intent to capture these memories and share them with my brothers and sisters so they would have a written account of my conversations with Mom and Dad.

When reading through the notes I realized that these were more than stories about my family. They were more than just random, or pointed conversations with my parents. They were a reflection of a child desperately grasping to hold on to his parents for as long as possible, especially as time rapidly slipped away.

My thoughts were broken when my brother Mike approached me and pointed out that the funeral home had put the wrong name up on the tribute video. It said, "Gerald" not "Gerard" McShane. I chuckled and walked over to the employee with whom we had planned the wake. He was very apologetic and rushed to correct the problem immediately. I thought, "That's the exact type of thing dad could not have cared less about."

My brothers and sisters, Mike, Jim, Marsha, Ed, Steve, Joyce and Maura, along with their families and my mom, all filed in before the wake was opened to the general public and extended family. As we had done the night before, we scattered about the room and did not form a "receiving line of death." With eight kids it's too much. We figured it was easier for folks to come in, do a quick viewing and find the person that they know to say how sorry they are and then they can easily escape.

The stories flowed easily at both wakes for my father. My siblings are great story tellers and so much of what they have seen unfortunately will not see the pages of this book. This story is centered on my conversations, experiences and, ultimately, one of my visits.

In May of 2016 my siblings and I first heard that Dad's health had taken a dramatic turn for the worse. Five of the eight kids had an opportunity to visit our parents together. Our visit was especially memorable and special.

The following pages talk about a family saying good bye to our Dad, our appreciation, laughter, and admiration.

The End... Sort of...

Since we began with the wake, we may as well continue on with the end before we get to the beginning.

When Dad passed, I was given the tremendous honor and responsibility of representing our family in eulogizing him at his service in Saint Charles Church in Waltham.

The following words may help you understand who he was before we take a step back and meet him.

This was Dad's Eulogy:

Before I begin, please take a moment to glance around at Saint Charles Church.

Both of my grandfathers, along with many other soon-to-be parishioners, helped excavate the land for Saint Charles using only shovels and wheelbarrows. My parents received their first communions here, they were confirmed here and they were married here. I just wanted everyone to appreciate the significance of our surroundings.

As your eyes face the altar you obviously notice the casket. With Mom's instructions regarding what she was looking for in-hand, Joyce and I went to the funeral home to review a few models and sent pictures down to Florida for Mom and Maura to make the final selection. Maura has been by Mom's side for everything over the last few months and we cannot thank you enough for all you have done.

Mom selected the casket you see in front of us. Maura replied that she really liked this one as well, however, she was a little concerned because the casket has gold on it and we need to remember that, "over time, gold will tarnish."

I asked permission before I told that story.

At the age of 16 my Dad brought me to a huge, empty parking lot to teach me how to drive. I immediately drifted to the far right-hand side where trees were overhanging the pavement.

My Father barked at me to get to the left but, with hands held firmly at 10 and 2, I only managed to straighten the car out and proceeded to rapidly drive straight down the row of trees.

Each leafy branch slapped against the windshield of the car and then wrapped inside the open passenger window and struck Dad in the face and upper torso region. Out of the corner of my eye, I saw him drop his chin into his chest and raise his arms as the onslaught of branches pummeled him into submission.

Whack, whack…whack, whack, whack…whack, whack. There was nowhere for him to hide.

I finally slowed the car to a stop and turned towards him. A lone branch stuck in through the passenger window. Dad's bald head and face were red with the blows from branches and his polo shirt had a smattering of leaves gently resting on his right shoulder and chest.

There were no words. He just looked at me. Bewildered. His eyes told me he truly wondered if I could really be his offspring.

I looked back and my only thought was that this man made it through World War II and I almost killed him with weeping willows.

My Father didn't need words, he was remarkably facially expressive. If you were paying attention you always knew where you stood.

If he looked straight on at you and laughed with one soft slap of his right hand on his right thigh or if he slightly nodded while following a serious conversation he was enjoying his time.

If he raised his eyebrows, pursed his lips, tilted his head to the side and nodded slightly it meant he either thought you were on the right track or you made him think about something.

If his eyebrows were down, his eyes were squinted and he wore a pained, closed-lip grin and he breathed deeply through his nose it meant he knew you meant well but you were missing something that he found to be fairly obvious.

If he shook his tilted head with eyes closed and gave an exasperated laugh which ended in a small sigh it meant that you were missing something that he now determined you were never going to understand.

He was this extraordinary blend of utter confidence and complete humility. He was not intimidated by anything or anyone but NEVER spoke of all he accomplished. I struggled with how to try to honor him today. I felt that by getting up here and speaking of some of his accomplishments was almost a betrayal of how he conducted his life. However, if I don't say them now, who will? And some of these are too great not to share. So, on that note:

Did you know:

His high school football coach said he could arrange for my Father to receive a four-year scholarship to play football at Holy Cross, but Dad respectfully declined. It would have meant deferring going into the Marines to serve his country in World War II.

Did you know:

In the War he crossed enemy lines, disobeying direct orders from his superior officer, so he could put another Marine on his back during an intense battle and carry him to safety, saving that Marine's life.

During another battle he was in a fox hole with his sergeant and was struck by shrapnel and did not come to until he was on a boat receiving medical treatment. He never knew how he got to the boat but he knew his sergeant, somehow, saved his life.

My brother Mike worked tirelessly in the last months of Dad's life to try to get answers on how he was saved. Mike found the son of the other Marine and, it turns out, the man Dad shared a fox hole with, the man who saved his life, preceded my father in death by four-months. That reunion must have been amazing.

After spending a year in various hospitals following his war injury, he returned home at the age of 19, married Mom…on a Tuesday…because it was the slowest day of the week for McShane Oil. They cancelled classes at St. Charles so the upperclassmen could attend the wedding. He then purchased half of McShane Oil from his father. He bought out the rest of the business when his dad retired. He owned and operated McShane Oil until 1977.

I remember my parents sorting invoices and making a pile of notes that would go unpaid. As an eight year-old I questioned why they would continue to bring oil to people they knew couldn't pay their bills. Dad read the name off the top invoice and told me how she was in her 80s and widowed. How she barely had money to pay for her food. He read the second name and spoke of how that person had just lost his job. My parents looked at me and said, "If we don't help people in difficult situations, who will?" It was never about getting as much as you could. It was always about helping as much as you could.

Did you know:

For a brief period after McShane Oil, he owned a sub shop. I mention this because it gave birth to one of the all-time great lines when Mom said, "Gerard, you might be the first person who has ever owned a sub shop that has never made a sandwich."

He went to work for Bentley College as equipment manager. I ended up attending college there and was very wary about my dad cramping my style. Within a couple of months I realized that the quickest way I had of making friends was by saying, "I'm Jerry's son."

But that stuff is just a resume. My dad - my parents are anything but a resume. They built their lives around their family. While Mom was, and is, the rock of the family, Dad thrust his passions upon us. Whether it was learning to play poker for candy at the age of five, or sitting down to Marx Brothers and W.C. Fields movie marathons, we were always welcome to be a part of their world.

You have to understand, the eight of us were each given the perfect upbringing. We don't fight. We want to be together. Each of us has always aspired to be like our parents. People often say that you don't realize all that you have until it's gone. Not in our case. For decades, we have gathered…in pubs, racetracks and casinos throughout New England and Florida to discuss how much we appreciate all with which we have been blessed.

You want to honor my dad? Live as he lived.

Relax. Stop beating yourself up. Life is hard. You're doing fine.

Spend time with your family. Grab a deck of cards. Watch a movie. Play a game. Ask them how their day was and LISTEN when they respond. The eight of us always knew that we came first with our parents. Unless the Patriots, Red Sox or Celtics were on; then we were a distant, distant second.

Don't do things to impress other people. Do things because they are the right things to do.

You see, our dad is NOT gone.

Eat a Mr. Goodbar and it's gone. Drop 20 bucks on a horserace and it's gone.

But Dad isn't a product that was used and discarded. He was an educator, a friend, a supporter, a motivator and he was, is and forever will be our example. Someone who shapes who you are can never truly be gone.

Picture a mountain range or an ocean. Even if you know that you're never going to get to see that landscape again, that doesn't mean that it will ever be gone.

Our dad, our mountain, will NEVER, ever be gone.

Prologue

By 2016 Dad had been experiencing short-term memory loss for a couple of years. Mom was assisting him and covering-up for his deficiencies (as most caregiving spouses become adept at doing). His memory loss wasn't that bad. Yes, he had forgetful moments but he would laugh about most of them. My parents made jokes about senility seeping in and, when reminded of whatever had slipped his mind, he would either remember or own up to not having any recollection whatsoever. It was not anything remotely close to full-blown dementia. It was an annoyance that was fairly easily managed.

The immediate threat to his well-being was that he had extreme dizziness and balance issues that came on in his late 80s and worsened with each passing year. Whenever he stood or walked it was as if he was meandering across the deck of a ship at sea. There were no issues when he was seated or lying down. Over three years, Dad had seen a dozen doctors and specialists who had each proclaimed that they would be the one to figure out the root cause of his vertigo. None were able to diagnose the issue or provide a cure.

The family received regular updates about Dad's health but nothing was life-threatening, they were simply issues which needed to be addressed. Actually, the greater concern was for Mom and her ability to care for Dad if he fell. We talked about getting him a walker or a scooter but he scoffed at those recommendations.

His take was simple, *he was fine and he was always going to be fine.* He continued to walk without assistance and he continued to fall, again and again. Mom, at 94 pounds, would regularly be struggling to help him to his feet. They were each 90 years old.

Dad had a serious fall in March of 2016 that put him in a rehabilitation facility. I flew down and met my parents, my sister Maura, my brother Mike and his wife Ann to take a look at a senior living community in Clearwater, Florida. During our visit we spoke with an elder law attorney to make sure my parents had the proper paperwork for Durable Power of Attorney and Health Care Proxy in case of an emergency.

I flew home with a solid plan in place. Mom and Dad were placing a deposit on a two-bedroom villa at a beautiful senior living community, located a few miles from where they lived. Unfortunately, they never made it to that community. A week after leaving rehab, Dad fell again. This put him back in the hospital with a long-term prognosis of needing to live in a skilled nursing facility. He had good days but, more-and-more, his quality of life was below average. There were enough scares that we all started taking a deep breath whenever we received a call from a family member. We were all well aware that the end could come at any time.

An email from Maura informing us that Dad was not eating and refusing his feeding tube made us see the end might be imminent. The email read:

Hi,

For those of you that called me this morning and wanted to fly out. I would plan on doing that at your earliest convenience. Since this morning Dad had been choking on all food and liquids and he needs a feeding tube that he refused to have. He is alert and answering all the questions. I can accommodate everyone at my house that wants to come. Just let me know. The only plan for him right now is hospice.

The only plan for him right now is hospice? The **ONLY** plan for him right now is hospice. Those are the only words I could see. The **ONLY** plan for **HIM** right now is **HOSPICE**. A follow-up email detailed the reasons behind the recommendation for him to be put on hospice services. It was said he should be placed in a hospice house where he *may* only have from five to seven days left to live.

Some of my siblings had just been down to Florida and others had a trip already scheduled for a couple of weeks from the date of the email. Maura lived 20 minutes from my parents. Four of us decided that we would fly down from Massachusetts within the next 36 hours.

I decided to leave the next morning and jumped online to book my flight. The toughest part was scheduling the return trip home. My employer was remarkably compassionate, I was instructed to take a week, a month, whatever I needed. The situation took precedent over any and all projects and assignments.

The fact is, though, life doesn't stop. I have a wife and children, commitments and obligations. This could not be an open-ended journey because we all know that end-of-life doesn't follow regimented guidelines. It can come in an instant or it can linger for periods of time far longer than what was originally anticipated. There had to be a return trip scheduled.

I would travel to Florida the next day, Thursday morning, and would return home the following Monday evening. I would have five days in Florida.

Five days left with Dad.

Chapter 1

I set the alarm for 4:40 a.m. While giving the appearance of sleeping, I just laid on my left side, trying hard to keep my eyes shut but they constantly blinked open staring into the vast darkness of my bedroom.

There was an edginess to the night, an unyielding worry that a ringing phone would cut through the silence informing me that Dad passed in his sleep. At 4:05 a.m. I ended the charade of pretending to sleep and got out of bed, reaching instinctively for the bed post while making my way in the dark until I found the bathroom door handle.

I shaved, showered, dressed, went down to the kitchen and poured a bowl of Cheerios. No different than every other morning. My senses were shut down, I wasn't registering any taste. I just stared blankly at the glass sliding door that leads from our kitchen to the three-season room. Upon completion, I picked up the bowl and spoon and walked over and placed them in the sink. Even in times of grief, my dishes do not make it all the way into the dishwasher.

I trudged up the staircase and reentered my bedroom. I lifted my suitcase from the floor and set it on the hamper to review its contents one last time.

Theresa, stood in the bedroom door, holding a pile of mail that had found its way to her nightstand from one of her many late night bill paying sessions she does while sitting up in our bed. While she shares some of my Irish heritage, the blood that flows through Theresa's veins is mainly from Italy where end of life situations can certainly be filled with far more outpourings of grief and sorrow than what the Irish like to present. These conflicting emotions led Theresa to appear tense and uncomfortable, as if she was trying to meet me at my stage of grief rather than showing hers. "Do you need me to take care of anything when you're away?" she asked.

"I don't think so," I said without thought, slightly shaking my head and not making eye contact. I then stopped and shrugged. With a sigh I continued, "I guess we should just be prepared for everyone to come up here from Florida in the next couple of weeks. But I don't really know what we can do to prepare for that right now."

"No problem," she said. "I'll get the house ready. Well, I'll try to get the house ready." Three teenage daughters have a way of cutting a never-ending path of destruction through a home. Piles of laundry, schoolwork and dishes await you at every turn, and even when the house gets a thorough once-over, it is destroyed in a matter of hours by the whirlwind hurricane McShane.

"Thanks," I muttered.

She hesitated as if not wanting to say something and stared at me while I was finishing packing my luggage. I looked over at her. She put down the mail on our bureau and began collecting dress shirts and a pair of her pants. Theresa casually said, "I'm going to the dry-cleaners, if you need anything done there?"

"Just my shirts," I said, motioning towards what she already had in her arms.

"Ok," she responded hesitantly and continued to gather clothes. "Nothing else?"

Her gentle guidance finally resonated, I went into our closet and my eyes drifted, purposefully, across my clothes. I gently tugged my dark gray and navy pin stripe suits off their hangers and placed them on top of the pile of clothes being brought in for cleaning.

"Thank you," I softly said. Her response was a simple, caring nod. Words were tough to formulate at this moment. How do you handle the mundane tasks when a monumental shift to your life is about to occur?

This was surreal; we knew even if Dad passed over the next few days there would be time for all of this but we were still trying to put everything in order. There was some discussion around preparation but it was minimal, mainly just actions showing that we were getting ready for a gathering. In case the inevitable occurred soon, the focus would be on family and not on a to-do list.

We were running early (we never run early) and did not need to leave for another 15 minutes to pick up two of my brothers, Jim and Steve. I went into the living room and sat on the couch while Theresa jotted down a note to leave on the kitchen counter for the kids. My eyes focused on my piece of blue luggage. My thoughts drifted to seeing my Dad this afternoon. What was I supposed to say? How was I supposed to greet him?

In the movies there are sweeping heartfelt emotions and the deliverance of messages that had been repressed for years. Our family is very close but we only have the ability to show two emotions: humor 85% of the time and frustration 15% of the time. Other than that, we are superstars at avoiding confrontation or uncomfortably sad moments. We are old school Irish. Bad things happen and the only way to get through is with a joke.

Did the gravity of this situation call for a different protocol? Should the visit be humor infused or would I forever regret not saying "the important stuff"? When we walked in, everyone in that hospital room including – especially – Dad was going to know why we all suddenly appeared at his bedside in Clearwater, Florida. Did this need to be verbally addressed or could it just be silently understood? Please, please, please let it be silently understood. Would he directly question us regarding why we decided now was the ideal time to visit? I had no answers; there was nothing with which I could compare this situation.

I hoped everything would just flow naturally. My thoughts went from Dad to a horrible professional moment in my career when I was given the assignment of flying from Massachusetts to Washington DC with a co-worker to close a branch office of a business. We dreaded every second of how the conversations would play out, and what short and long-term ramifications we would be imposing on the lives of those talented and hard-working individuals losing their positions.

We arrived at the office, unannounced, at 9:05 a.m. on a Monday morning. As we turned the corner, our receptionist glanced up, flipped his pen in the air, stood and turned around to the open bullpen area layout where our employees all worked. "That's it everyone," he yelled. "We're all fired." While it was not how we had mapped out these conversations, it certainly added immediacy to an extremely uncomfortable situation.

So much of me hoped that Dad would handle this situation in the same manner as that 23 year-old receptionist. Address it quickly and put it on the table. If he didn't, I had no idea how the conversation, or if the conversation, would take place. All I was sure of was that if things got too uncomfortable, my plan was to hide behind my older brothers and let them figure it out.

Chapter 2

Patrick Joseph McShane, my grandfather on Dad's side, was born in 1895 in Belfast, Ireland.

Poor laborers, like the McShanes, were being devastated by the potato famine and the black plague. While the lace-curtain Irish would complain about having to do without, the shanty-Irish drifted off to sleep each evening wondering if they would have the luxury of waking up in the morning.

Failed economic policies of the Irish government exported much of the grain from the country, leaving many starving citizens in the streets. There was not enough work, food or money to sustain the McShane family. They huddled together, discussing any solutions to either save or, at least, extend their lives.

My grandfather's aunt left Ireland for America a few years earlier. She was planning a return to take care of some business and the family pleaded with her to take some of their children back with her to the States. She could only accommodate one, it was determined that would be Patrick Joseph.

It was 1907, Patrick Joseph was not able to find work at the age of 12 and the family could not afford another mouth to feed. His aunt graciously brought the young boy back to her home in Waltham, Massachusetts, a city that stretches out along the Charles River about 11 miles northwest of downtown Boston. He was scared and did not want to leave his native land, where his immediate family remained and his friends filled his head with how poorly the Irish were treated in the States.

The young boy was alone in this new world. He knew of his new-found family but did not know them. Adults had told him positive stories of Boston but he had never heard of Waltham. If it was his choice, he would have stayed in Belfast and bet on his abilities to find some work, somewhere. The choice was not his. His parents knew this was his best opportunity at survival.

Like most immigrants, Patrick Joseph was welcomed to the United States with unopened arms. Not-so-subtle barbs crashed against him like left crosses and right uppercuts. He was nothing more than just another "Mick" or "Paddy" to the well-established Boston Brahmins. Even though he was a mere youth, he was categorized with the other recent immigrants from the Emerald Isle as a rampaging hoard of violent alcoholics who would delight equally in cracking a joke or a skull.

Patrick Joseph quickly befriended other Irish youths who were also discarded by those with assets and power. These scared and misplaced adolescents had been shipped from their homeland to live with a mishmash of relatives and caregivers as their families searched for answers in Ireland. The children gathered in playgrounds and on streets away from stores where shopkeepers mistrusted the poor youths who, they felt, must only be entering for the opportunity to steal as they obviously had no money to pay.

These children vowed to one another that they would lead a better life than what they had experienced to this point. They were raised in the Church and at home to be polite, respectful and tough. They trusted Catholics, specifically Irish Catholics. All other religions and nationalities had sent them a clear message, they were nothing more than a collection of poor mutts running wildly in the street and times were better before they had arrived.

My grandfather began going by his middle name, Joseph, because the prejudices against the Irish were so strong that he tried desperately to gain some traction wherever he could. Any distance he could place between himself and the "Paddy" moniker could only help his chances of gaining and keeping employment.

The deep resentment of having to hide their heritage weighed on these children. There was no melting pot, there was no fitting in, these youths who were well regarded in Ireland were disregarded in America. They knew they were not wanted by anyone other than each other. They would feel the glares burrowing into their skin and hear the voices imploring them to return to their homeland to a certain death.

In the late afternoon and early evening hours these bands of Irish youth would gather to play soccer or baseball. Soccer was more common because it only required a ball and they could usually scrounge one up. Baseball was trickier as most of these children could not afford mitts so they would handle sharp line drives by swatting the ball down with their non throwing hand so they could pick the ball up then throw it to first while rapidly shaking their recently scorched hand with the hope that the blazing sting would cease.

On weekends they met at Mass. Every day they would knock the heads off orange flowers because they thought Protestants were growing them as yet another way to taunt the Catholics.

My grandfather anxiously awaited the move of his parents and siblings so he could rejoin his family. By the time his family saved enough money to make the journey to the United States, the desolate conditions had claimed the lives of his father and sister, each of them dying in Ireland.

Chapter 3

Theresa drove through a misty, cool, May morning, the first of what was forecasted to be a week of miserable days for Massachusetts. We picked up my brother Steve and then swung over and got Jim. She navigated through light traffic to the shuttle which would bring us into Logan Airport in Boston.

Jim and Steve sat next to each other on the bus and I sat against the window across the aisle. Travelers to Logan filed onto the shuttle. One sat in the aisle seat next to me which prohibited my ability to talk with my brothers on the way to the airport. I was more than satisfied with the seating arrangement as I still wanted an opportunity to work through all that had transpired over the last 24 hours. There would be plenty of time to speak with them over the next five days.

Unfortunately, my newly-acquired seat mate was a bubbly, excited woman who appeared to be in her early 60s and she desperately wanted someone with whom to speak. She turned to me a couple of times with a smile and provided me numerous conversation starters such as, what a cool morning it was; how surprised she was at the crowd on the shuttle at 6:00 a.m. and how she was anxious to get away for a week and just forget about the day-to-day grind. I politely nodded and slightly grinned but kept my focus directly on the screen of my phone.

It was early but I sent a text message to three friends with whom I had grown up. Two were unaware of any health concerns with Dad. The other knew there were issues but had no idea how bad things had become. Until 18 hours ago, none of us had known of the severity.

My text simply read:

> *I am heading to catch a plane to Tampa right now. My father's health has declined rapidly. He is being put on hospice. We are expecting him to pass quickly. Probably days, maybe weeks. I apologize for the informality of letting you know by text. It's very hectic and I am rushing for the plane. I will call you when I can.*

There was nothing hectic about the situation. Actually, my life was moving along methodically with vast amounts of downtime. Even as I typed those words into my phone all I was doing was sitting alone on a bus. I knew I could type the words describing Dad's rapidly declining medical situation but I did not want to hear those words being said by my voice. Nor did I want to have to answer questions with guesses or to hear optimistic tones of someone telling me that they knew someone who was put on hospice that lasted for years or people trying to convince me that doctors can be wrong. Yes, all those things can happen and have happened but I was working pretty hard to acclimate to the thought of life without Dad. I was in no mood of anyone filling my head with a false sense of hope. If a miracle was going to occur, I'd rather be surprised.

The woman next to me kept giving me sideways grins and little nods of welcome. She gave all the appearances of being a nervous traveler. I shut off my phone as we were passing the campus of Boston University.

I needed a break from my thoughts.

"They're out early," I said, giving my fellow passenger an opening, as I motioned down to the Boston University players practicing on Nickerson Field.

"I was just thinking the same thing," she said enthusiastically. "Imagine doing that and then having to go to class all day - then they're probably right back on the field in the afternoon!"

I grinned, nodded and then looked straight ahead at the blueish/purple back of the seat cushion in front of me. The design was adorned with slight, colorful swirls.

"I love traveling but I'm not too crazy about the flying part," she continued.

I nodded, dropped my eyebrows to create a furrowed brow, slightly frowned and glanced her way. I shrugged, "It's just like being on this bus except a little higher up."

"The little higher up part is what makes me nervous," she said with a laugh.

I gave a slight laugh.

She smiled, "Are you traveling for business or pleasure?"

Neither.

"I'm going down to see my parents in Florida."

"Nice," she said with a tilt of her head and her voice rising to help share in the excitement that she obviously felt that I should have. "That should be fun," she said in a convincing fashion.

For the first time in my life I could not use the word "fun" to describe my trip to Florida.

I simply said, "I'm looking forward to seeing them."

Chapter 4

The Brahmins' fears started becoming realized. As more and more Irish flooded the Waltham area, the Mayflower descendants (or Mayflower descendent posers) began to take flight to less culturally diverse suburbs. The Irish made gains in government jobs and in working on the lines in local factories.

"The 'non-immigrant crowds,' - immigrants themselves who just beat the Irish to the United States by a few decades, "Cared as much about us as they cared about stray dogs," my grandfather had said to my dad later in life. "Actually, that's not fair. They probably did care about stray dogs. They had no use at all for us."

After being turned away by every "respectable" person of influence in their region, the Irish began to build symbolic walls around themselves… not that anyone was trying to enter those social circles anyway. They kept relationships amongst themselves. They supported each other professionally and socially.

They followed the lead of Boston's Mayor James Michael Curley. The people's mayor. The underlying thought was if the Irish could take over politics and the police force, those who wanted to keep them down would be hard pressed to stop their advances. They knew they would never be welcomed at the old, stodgy Boston men's clubs littered with bankers and investment managers. But that wasn't a concern. The thought was if they carried the same size stick the odds of getting beat down became significantly less.

My grandfather was not a politician and did not enter into law enforcement but he did have dreams on starting his own business and capitalizing on the Irish first sentiments of his fellow countrymen. He also followed the proper protocol when he met, fell in love and married Teresa Hardiman. Teresa was born in Waltham in 1900. Her parents had escaped the famine just a few years prior from Galway, Ireland. While America wasn't home, those in the Galway, Aran Islands area of Ireland did feel a sense of comfort with Massachusetts. They liked to say that the next Parish to the West was in Boston.

For the time being, Joseph worked any and all jobs that may have been available. "I remembered what it was like to be hungry," he said. "I was still hungry. Times were better in America but we were living in poverty. It just felt like we were on top of the world considering what we came from."

After a couple of years, Joseph landed a line job at The Waltham Watch Company which was the number one employer of laborers in the Waltham region (it was nicknamed St. Charles College as most of the students coming out of the local Catholic school, both graduates and dropouts, ended up working on the lines). Joseph's education went until the 5th grade, Teresa's went until the 8th. They had three daughters and one son, Gerard, my dad.

Mom's family had a slightly easier transition into the States. Having come over earlier and they traveled all together and not piecemeal. They were either going to all make it or perish together.

Mom's family immigrated to America from Belfast, Ireland in the 1880s. Her father, Edward Vallely was born in Clinton Massachusetts in 1892. Her mother, Mary Maher, was born in Waltham in 1894.

Edward and Mary met while they worked at the Waltham Watch Company. When they met, Mary was engaged to another man, Jack Doucette. "I never cared for him very much," she had said, "but I talked myself into believing that maybe love would grow in time."

"He surprised me," she said. "Jack just walked in to work one day, pulled a small box from his pocket and showed me the engagement ring he had purchased for me."

He stood there, smiled and said, "Mary, will you be my bride?"

Mary was dumbfounded, she looked at the ring for a few moments and thoughts rushed through her head. She certainly wasn't in love but he wasn't a bad man and she mused that he, at least, must love her. She felt that life could be worse. She said a very unenthusiastic, "Yes."

Within a couple of months she met Edward and quickly realized she had no (positive) feelings for Jack. "I went right to him and told him the relationship was through. It was hard to hurt someone but I knew that I had met the man that I was going to marry and it was not Jack."

Unfortunately, Jack was smitten and never saw it coming. "He tried desperately to overcome my rejection but my mind and heart were set on Edward." Mary and Edward married in 1916 and had seven children, four boys and three girls, including Florence, my mom.

The oldest boy, Edward (Jr.), died in the hospital slightly before his second birthday as a nurse went from wing to wing checking on patients and carried an infectious disease in to him. Mom's father, Edward, died in 1932 from cancer, leaving her Mother alone to raise the six surviving children.

Mom was born on June 3, 1925 and lived at 63 Taylor Street in Waltham. Dad was born a few weeks later, on June 27 and lived two houses off Moody Street in Waltham at 86 Cherry Street. They grew up six-blocks apart and attended the same school since first grade but didn't meet until high school because Mom started school a year before Dad.

Chapter 5

Jim, Steve and I plodded through security at Logan Airport and stopped at a bookstore so Jim could grab something to read on the plane. I glanced in the direction of the business books but no words or titles were registering in my head.

My phone buzzed with a return call from one of the friends I had texted earlier. I watched the screen, contemplating if I dared pick it up and, potentially, show true emotion.

"Hey, I'm going down to Dunks (Dunkin' Donuts) to grab a coffee and a bagel," Steve said breaking the silence. A diversion, perfect, I had an excuse to ignore the call.

"What?" Jim said looking up from a book he was thumbing through.

"I'm going to Dunks," Steve repeated. "You want anything?"

"Yeah, I'll take a regular coffee, thanks," Jim said.

"Patrick, anything?" Steve said as I looked down at my phone which had just notified me that I received a voicemail.

"Yeah, um, a hot chocolate. Please. Thanks," I said.

Jim glanced at me, squinting with a condescending grin. He looked back at Steve, gave a slight eyebrow raise, and they both laughed.

"A hot chocolate," Steve repeated.

"A hot chocolate," I said. My eyes darted back and forth from one brother to the other. Not the first time that I've been called out on the fact that my taste buds haven't changed very much from when I was eight years old.

The three of us stood facing each other. There was no need at all to defend my preference. So, with that in mind, I quickly defended my preference. "It tastes better than coffee. You don't have to give up the good stuff because you got old."

My defense did not win over any supporters. "Do you want whipped cream with that?" Steve asked with eyes open wide and nodding at me like I was four.

Jim laughed.

The mocking joke was a delicious reminder. Oh how I love my hot chocolate with (in order of preference) Fluff, marshmallows or whipped cream. As Steve turned to get our drinks I muttered, "Yeah, I do."

Steve head slowly turned back and he looked at me.

"I do," I repeated. "I want the whipped cream too." Steve gave a small laugh before turning back around to get the drinks.

Jim laughed and started to check out some books on a display facing out into the hall. I gave up on the idea of reading and started checking out snacks.

I love airports for two reasons. 1. People watching is great theater. 2. As soon as you enter an airport all rules of what you are supposed to eat and drink are completely abandoned. The airport is the only place where a bag of Fritos, a King Size Snickers bar and a Diet Coke counts for a perfectly acceptable breakfast.

Steve returned with our drinks and we walked through the terminal, went down an escalator, walked through a couple of long hallways (on those automated people moving ramps) and rode up another escalator before reaching our gate. All the while, we shared stories about Dad. I had heard most of them before, a few were new, and a couple had variations on how I remembered and told them.

Jim and Steve sat at the gate as I paced back and forth in the aisle in front of them. While there were certainly nerves involved with my pacing on this day, it is normal for me to walk a lot, especially if I know that I'm going to be confined to a seat for a period of hours.

As the minutes passed our boarding was called. All this time I had been receiving and sending text messages. As I was about to get on the plane, one message was more jarring than the rest. It had referred to Dad in the past tense. *"Your father was a great man..."*

I stopped abruptly causing a mini pile up of travelers to uncomfortably gather right behind me as I reread the text. I could hear the silent urging of all those who wanted me to walk forward the three additional feet I could move before I again would have to stop immediately behind my brother Steve.

If my father *was* a great man I wouldn't be in an airport right now rushing to get to Florida. If my father *was* a great man I would be home with my family sorting through issues of what I had or had not said to him over all of these years. If my father *was* a great man, my thoughts would almost be solely with my mother right now.

Nope, my father wasn't a great man. My father is a great man. I'm going to see him now.

Chapter 6

Mom and Dad were each four when the world got turned upside down from the Great Depression.

"In a lot of ways, the Depression was the great equalizer," Dad said many years later. "Lots of us never had anything. When the Depression was going on it felt like no one had anything."

There was no feeling of being deprived because most families did not have a phone or a car. "Everyone we knew struggled with paying bills and putting food on the table," Dad said. "We were poor. We were dirt poor for a long time but we never felt poor. We felt like everyone else. I guess that's because everyone else was also dirt poor."

They were instructed to find ways to entertain themselves, which led Mom, at the age of four, to put a paper bag over her head, spin in circles and then attempt to dizzily walk around the outside of her house. This was great fun until she wandered into the street. She could hear brakes screeching and felt the impact of a Model-T Ford striking her.

The man driving the car jumped out and ran around the vehicle. "Are you alright?" he stammered.

Mom was groggy but raised her head from the pavement. She was not crying but was probably in a state of shock. She hazily said, "I think so."

"Good, good," the man said quickly as he rifled through his pockets. "Here's what we'll do, I'll give you this quarter if you promise to never, ever tell anyone, okay?"

Mom sat on the pavement and stared blankly at him.

"Okay?" He repeated a bit louder and with more force.

"Okay," she repeated.

He pressed the quarter into her small hand, jumped back into his car and sped off down the street.

That same year, 1929, my paternal grandfather came to the realization that there was no way he could support his growing family with the $24 a week he earned at The Watch Factory. He took his life savings of $250 and bought a truck.

"I did everything from move furniture to deliver coal," Joseph said. "It was what I had thought of years earlier. The Irish and my fellow Parishioners would want to help support my efforts to create a better life for me and my family. We all pulled for each other to get ahead."

Joseph developed a harness in the garage where he would stand alone and hoist off the back of the truck he used to to run a moving business and would replace it with the tank for oil and an area for ice. He purchased 300 pound blocks of ice for 50 cents each and would break them up and sell them to individuals for their refrigeration units. "Five or ten cents of profit here and there would add up over time," Joseph said.

Business was excruciatingly difficult to come by initially. "While people wanted to help me and support my business," Joseph said, "None of them had any money either." Joseph worked tirelessly trying to carve out a customer base but was often frustrated by the meager sums of money he was making. Six blocks down the road the story was no different with Mom's parents and their family.

The pain felt by parents who know that they cannot provide for their children is generally far greater than the pain felt by children not knowing what they were missing.

Chapter 7

Our plane touched down at Indianapolis International Airport for a half-hour stopover. Eight passengers were continuing on to Tampa. We were not changing planes.

As soon as the plane landed, we each grabbed our phones to check for any updates that may have occurred during the first leg of our flight.

There was no new information from Florida but there was an email to the family from Jim's son, Brian. It read:

> *The book, "Teammates" tells a story of Johnny Pesky, Bobby Doerr and Dom Dimaggio heading down to Florida to visit Ted Williams in what looked to be some of his last days....I can't help but think of that book right now.*
>
> *Today three great men are getting on a plane to visit another WWII Purple Heart recipient, and true American hero on what could be his last days. God bless all 8 of you as these days come closer. Grandpa is a great husband, father, and grandfather to all of us. His work ethic and dedication to family are things we all have learned from. A true champion of the American dream, by starting his own successful business*

and providing a great life for his family. Both Grandpa and Grandma are so strong, clearly that has rubbed off on their children as well, and I hope I can carry on that same strength when teaching our kids what it takes to be the best they can be.

We are all praying hard for all of you and wish we could be there as well.

-bri

We were all in agreement regarding the greatness of our dad. However, none of us considered ourselves to be great men. At this moment-in-time, we were just kids. It didn't matter that we were kids that were aged 69, 62 and 49. We were just kids wanting to get to our dad.

Chapter 8

When kids grow up with nothing, they tend to make the most of what is available to them. Mom and Dad were no different.

When school ended, they burst from the doors of St. Charles and tore down the streets to their respective homes where they rapidly changed clothes and bound out into the road to play. "The last thing you wanted to do was hang around the house," Mom said. "That was a sure way to be assigned additional chores."

In the winter the majority of St. Charles' students would meet daily to go ice skating at a no-charge, open-air rink located two blocks from Mom's house. In the summer they rented bikes for 10 cents an hour and regularly went swimming at various ponds in the area. The common denominators were always low-cost activities that could accommodate a large number of kids.

Children would run down to Moody Street which, at the time, was so packed on the weekends that you couldn't walk down the left hand side of the road. "No families that we hung around with could afford a car," Dad said. "You wanted to get somewhere you walked. If you needed to get somewhere in a hurry, you ran."

Babe Ruth, who lived west of Waltham in Sudbury, used to come down to Moody Street to do his shopping. "I would walk up and down that street over and over," Dad said. "Just trying to get a glimpse of Ruth. I never did. I just missed him a couple of times."

The stop on Moody Street for anyone with a sweet tooth was Candyland. Boris was the owner / operator. He sold (inarguably according to those that ate there) the best ice cream in the Commonwealth and ruled his shop with an iron-fist. Boris demanded that all who entered Candyland remain on their best behavior. If you talked too loud he would tell you to be quiet. If you persisted, you were banned from the store forever.

When Jerry Seinfeld created the Soup Nazi character in his show, Dad leaned forward in his chair laughing and pointed at the tv, he exclaimed, "That's Boris!" Dad was sent to Candyland every Saturday night for two quarts. That ice cream was like gold to everyone in that house and it was carefully rationed out to ensure no one received more than their fair share. It usually didn't make it past Tuesday and then there was that agonizing wait until they could afford to purchase two more quarts.

When not playing, all these kids were working. Tasks needed to get done so families could survive. When Dad turned 12, his father would have him drive the McShane Oil truck around the property for loading and unloading. He would extend his legs completely out straight in order to reach the gas and clutch. When he went for his license at 16, the instructor asked him to pull over two minutes into the test.

"So," the instructor said, "you've only been driving for a few months now, huh?"

Dad nervously nodded.

"Okay," the instructor said with a laugh as he filled out and handed Dad his license. "Well, I guess you're a natural."

My parents' childhood was normal and uncomplicated, filled with the challenges of the times but also surrounded by supportive and caring families. Their worlds did not extend too far outside the Waltham property line but they didn't need to; they had everything they wanted within a few blocks of Moody Street.

Chapter 9

Upon arrival at Tampa International airport, Jim received a strange, upbeat, text from his son Kevin commenting about the "great email about Grandpa." Steve opened the email on his phone, it was from Maura. Steve read it out loud to us.

> *Some really good news! The dr asked me this morning if we wanted a swallow study done. I told her yes. I figured it couldn't hurt and we could find out if he could eat ANYTHING on his own. I told the dr if mom didn't want it done I would let her know. Mom agreed. We just found out he can eat soft foods!!!!!!! We are so happy!!!! He wanted an Ensure earlier this morning and we had to say no. This is a great step! Now, we just need to see how much he is willing to eat on his own!*

We stood in the airport terminal glancing at one-another, optimistic but slightly confused. Jim broke the silence saying, "Should we grab a flight home and come back when it's more serious?"

We walked through the airport to the shuttle that would take us to the car rental talking about how we now had no idea what to expect when we came face-to-face with Dad. However, we refused to allow optimism to spread too much, reminding one another that his eating was just one challenge. Dad also had bleeding to the brain and other issues which still kept him on the critical list. Some came about through his numerous falls, while we were all unsure of the origin of other challenges.

While the fact that he could consume soft-foods was now telling us that there may be additional time, we were still dealing with an end-of-life situation. We had received an email from Maura two days prior with a picture of Dad lying in his hospital bed. He did not look good. We quickly came back to reality.

Steve's phone buzzed with a text from Maura. It said that Dad was questioning why everyone is coming down. Mom and Maura told him that it was a regularly scheduled visit for Steve and Jim and that I was coming down because of work. For 20 years that would have been a perfectly reasonable excuse as I had worked for a high-tech public relations agency and then in healthcare and traveled quite often. However, a year-ago I switched careers and was now the head of business development for a Boston based commercial painting company.

"What??!!" I exclaimed. "What kind of business am I supposed to have in Tampa?"

Jim and Steve both laughed.

"Tell Dad there was a wall that you needed to get to," Jim said.

"He is still with it," I said exasperated. "And now I'm put in a position of saying I had to swing down to Florida to grab a couple of gallons of semi-gloss."

The drive to the hospital continued with more jokes and lighthearted ribbing of each other…okay, of me. Any experienced poker player would be able to read all the tells in these facades. If we are stressed and experiencing high levels of anxiety, we are joking and pretending that nothing fazes us.

Chapter 10

Mom wasn't sure why she agreed to attend some random birthday party for a kid who was a year younger than her. Granted, the school was small and you tended to make friends outside of your grade more than if you had larger class sizes. Anyway, she didn't have anything else going on this Saturday night and her friends were going.

She was in 9th grade and talking to friends who had sat down moments earlier. She did not notice that another partygoer angled his way through the room toward her.

"Florence," a friend said, "this is Gerard McShane." She didn't know him but had seen him around the school. She knew he was in the 8th grade and she quickly realized he had more interest in speaking with her than she had in speaking with him. He seemed nice but she had no desire to go out with a younger boy.

Hours passed and the party was going to be coming to an end soon. Dad remained fixated on Mom. "I'm going to ask her out," he commented to no one in particular. Saying this so others could hear removed the opportunity to get cold feet.

There was a "go-for-it" murmuring of support. He took a deep breath and traversed the room, cloaking himself in false courage. Her internal objections were not verbalized. She accepted and their first date was the following week when they attended a St. Charles High School basketball game. They were 13 years old.

The awkward stupidity of adolescence is not something that was invented in later years; it has gone on since the dawn of man. Dad would stand on the corner and throw pebbles at Mom's second story window. Mom sat in her room hearing the clinking and clanging of rocks pelting agains the side of her house and her window panes. She would not immediately acknowledge these actions because she never wanted to look like she was just sitting around anxiously awaiting his arrival. She remained seated, her shades drawn.

After a few minutes of this activity she would hear her mother's footsteps begin to ascend the steps leading from the kitchen. Her mother's voice would sharply pierce the silence and wrap up the narrow, curved staircase to Mom's room. "Florence, tell him to stop all that rock throwing. He's going to break a window."

Without a clear thought of something intelligent to say and being too scared to risk immediate and direct rejection, Dad's go-to move was to be a general nuisance. His young, developing brain thought that if he acted obnoxious and disruptive and she didn't immediately cast him off that she must really like him.

Dad walked the long way home when running errands or getting out of school so he could rest on the side steps of Mom's house with a couple of his buddies. They spoke loudly of school and sports. Dad would bound up and down the few stairs raucously ensuring that Florence knew he was out there. He would uproariously laugh in exaggerated tones with the hope that she would not be able to resist all the fun taking place right outside her door.

Mom knew the angle he was playing and would sit inside and let him play the fool. She wanted to be out there with him but she didn't (she couldn't) give him the satisfaction of knowing that he coaxed her out of her house.

Mom's grandfather also lived in the two-family dwelling and after a while he would call her over to his side of the house and simply say, "Florence, get that little boy to go home. He is loud and bothers all of us."

His juvenile behavior did not deter her, however, and Mom and Dad would see each other every day, most of the time to simply walk and talk. If they were fortunate enough to have one cent in their pocket, they bought two caramels and walked from Waltham to Watertown.

Mom and Dad spent every free moment they had together throughout high school, even though there was opposition to their relationship. Dad was viewed as someone who would go on to marry and raise a family but members of the clergy had different plans for Mom. Many in the administration were trying to help amplify the Lord's calling so Mom would get the message that she would be a wonderful candidate for a life devoted to God.

The competition for Mom's future came to a head in high school when she and Dad were cast to be in a play opposite one-another. Dad wanted no part of participating in anything relating to drama. Sister Annata, who really liked Mom and Dad, assisted Dad in finagling his way out of performing.

Sister Tresilla, who really liked Mom and had no use for Dad because he was leading her astray from becoming a nun, boiled over with anger. Sister Tresilla exploded into a heated argument with Sister Annata regarding this just being one more example of Dad muddling the communication that Mom would have otherwise been receiving from God. Sister Annata would hear none of it and stood by her decision. In retaliation, Sister Tresilla sent priests to Mom's home to encourage her to follow the path God wanted most for her.

At the age of 16, and being a devout Catholic, the squad of nuns and priests which came together to recruit my mother to the order must have felt an awful lot like a calling. This was a time when the cloth equated to doing no wrong and their words were viewed as a continuation of Sunday's gospel.

There could not have been a more noble calling at the time than holy orders and there was not a parent at St. Charles who would not have beamed at the opportunity to say that while their friends children chose wealth, fame or glory, their child was personally called from God to help those in need.

While each of my parents embraced the teachings of Catholicism, Mom knew that a collection of nuns and priests from down the block did not constitute a calling. It was a group of people that she admired but there were other nuns and priests who let her know that she would know within her if she was supposed to go into the convent.

They each spent a lifetime loving their Catholicism. It was an inseparable part of who they were and how they lived. They embraced the teachings and protected the Church as if it was their child. Even in times of absolute crisis, they would deflect and defend until evidence was overwhelmingly against and, even at that point, they would be quick to point out that we were talking about a minority of bad people which you would find in any profession.

The defense wasn't done to minimize the actions of their Church. It was done to protect all the wonderful role models they had in the Church. It was done to point out that much good still remained even though a great evil had infested the ranks. It was done to justify the way they had lived their life and raised their children.

One of the first predators that was caught in the Church was a priest at St. Julia's in Weston, Massachusetts. The news hit especially close to home. That was our Parish and I had worked at that Church on weekends my freshman year in high school. When the story broke fifteen or so years later, my parents carefully questioned me about my experiences with that predator.

There was obvious relief that I was not a victim but also there was also a painstaking feeling of loss for these parents who were so protective of every aspect of their children's lives except for the one area where all Catholics had put their Faith in God. Something was stolen from all of us, those that left the Church and those that remained.

I still attend Mass each weekend. It feels more right than wrong. Although I'm not sure if that's because I feel that is where I want to be, where God wants me to be or if it's because that's where I know my parents would feel happiest with my decision.

Chapter 11

Mease Hospital in Clearwater looks like every hospital ever shown in a soap opera. The hospital is located right next to Westchester Gardens Health and Rehabilitation where Dad has been living during his recent struggles and less than two miles from Imperial Pines, the 55+ community where Mom and Dad had lived for the last 17 years.

I called Maura to tell her we were in the parking lot. She said she would meet us in the lobby to update us on all that was going on and to prepare us for what we were about to see.

Jim, Steve and I crossed through the parking lot in silence and entered the building through the main lobby doors. We glanced around and did not see elevators and stood outside the gift shop waiting apprehensively. A few moments later Maura came bounding around the corner. She greeted us, shrugged slightly with both palms raised toward the ceiling and slightly shook her head.

"It's been a tough week," she said. "But he did just start eating. I don't know what to tell you."

"We really appreciate the email heads-up," Steve said. "It's great that he's doing well."

She explained the situation in a little more detail and talked about the challenges that Dad had been facing and how he spent vast amounts of time in the hospital very disconnected. She said that Mom was very worn down and they were just trying to find the solutions to make him most comfortable.

"Let's go up," she said and everyone turned and began walking down the hallway.

"Wait a second," I cut everyone off. "Explain to me the reasons Dad was told why everyone was down here."

"It was a regularly scheduled visit for Jim and Steve and you just joined them because you were planning to come down sometime this month anyway," she said.

"Nothing about me having to come down for work?" I asked.

"Nope, just a regularly scheduled visit," she replied.

"Okay."

"We did tell him that people are nervous," Maura continued. "We told him that when he wasn't eating and refusing the feeding tube we had to take the situation seriously."

"What did he say when you said that?" Steve asked.

"He just nodded," Maura said with a slight grin, slight grimace. "Let's go up."

We all began walking towards the elevators. I was off the hook for an excuse as to why work needed me to swing by Florida. Now my earlier anxieties were resurfacing. What do you say to someone when you are very aware that there are only a finite number of conversations remaining?

Chapter 12

The City Lottery.

Money was tight (to clarify in this sentence the word "tight" means there was none) and everyone was looking for some way to get ahead. The City Lottery was an underground gambling operation that ran just as the numbers run today. You would wager, numbers would be drawn, and if you won, you were notified and paid.

The only differences between what is done today and what was done then is that this lottery was not legal and it was run primarily in the Black neighborhoods of Boston. Joseph knew someone who knew someone, and he worked up a dollar every now and again to drop a wager through a local oddsmaker.

One morning, as Joseph was unloading boxes from his truck, a voice cracked through the job's monotony.

"Joe!"

The booming voice startled him as he turned and saw the oddsmaker quickly approaching him.

"Joe," he called again and as he got closer he smiled broadly. "You won, Joe! You won!"

"I won what?" Joseph responded.

"The lottery! You won!"

He laughed and said, "Really? I won? How much?"

"$7,500."

Joseph stopped laughing. He leaned back against his truck in shock. He was expecting a few hundred. "You're serious?"

"I am!"

"You have the money?" He said with some nervousness in his voice. At that time his wages for the week would have been closer to $30. He had never had a net worth of $7,500 let alone held that much money in his hands.

"Oh I don't pay you. They do."

"Who does?"

"The ones who run the lottery." He then told my grandfather where to stand the following morning at 10:00 a.m. He said they would meet him there with his money.

Joseph was a bundle of nerves that night. Excited at the prospect of an incredibly large payout but fearful of everything that could go wrong, including getting robbed immediately after taking such a large sum of money into his possession. He didn't breathe a word about his winnings to anyone, including his wife, Teresa. He told her that he won but would not say how much. He hoped that the bookmaker would also keep his mouth shut.

The following morning, Joseph stood by the side of the road, as instructed, at 10:00 a.m. He nervously shifted from side to side. At a few minutes past the hour a sedan pulled up and a large Black man stepped out from the back.

"Are you Joseph McShane?"

Joseph nodded.

"Get in," the man said and motioned to the car. Joseph hesitated for a couple of moments. The large man stared at him. Against his better judgement, he got in the car and the man got in and sat next to him. Another Black man was driving the car. This was the first time in my grandfather's life that he had come in contact with people who were Black.

As the car was driving, the man in the back handed my grandfather a large piece of cloth and told him to tie it around his eyes. "Well, I'm dead," Joseph thought to himself. He glanced to the door and wondered if he should jump but what would that do? "Why would they kill me," he thought. "They could have just no-showed if they didn't want to pay me."

After a fairly lengthy drive, the car stopped and he was told to step out of the car but to leave the blindfold on. Joseph could tell from the sound the tires made on the crunching of leaves and the scent of pine and oak trees that they were somewhere in the woods.

The large man in the back got out of the car and walked around to Joseph's side. He opened Joseph's door, grabbed his arm and said, "Come with me." The driver's door never opened or shut.

"Where?" Joseph asked as he cautiously got out of the car.

"Come with me."

Again, there was no solution to the predicament that he put himself in, so he did as instructed. After walking for five minutes, they stopped. "Lift your blindfold up just enough to see and pick up the bag in front of you," the voice said from his rear.

Joseph slowly peeled the lower corner of his blindfold up, not only noticing a bag in front of him but also the corner of an oak desk with a leather chair. They had a full executive office set up in the middle of the woods. He reached down and grabbed the handles of the bag.

He felt the hand grab his left elbow. He clutched the bag tightly in his right hand as his body was turned and he began blindly walking back with the man who originally led him in. He heard movement but no voices behind him. There were at least two other individuals who were back in the office space who remained safely out of view. This added a level of comfort. "If they don't want me to see them," he thought, "they must expect me to make it home."

In silence, they drove back to the same corner where he was picked up. As the car pulled to a stop the man sitting next to Joseph said, "Turn to the door, remove your blindfold. Get out and don't look back."

"Okay," Joseph said and did as instructed, still clutching the bag in his right hand. He stepped out on to the curb and began quickly walking towards his vehicle. He heard the car pull away behind him.

He hadn't cheated death but there was a feeling like he did. There was a moment of driving home with more money in his pocket than he had managed to save throughout a lifetime.

As he walked through the door he called into the kitchen, "Teresa, I've got something to show you."

He impatiently waited. Kids played outside but he felt best that they not know. The less people talking about the windfall, the better. Teresa came into the room and he said, "You know how I told you I had hit the lottery?"

She nodded.

He pulled a wad of bills out of his pocket and spread them out across the table.

She stared at the bills and then back at him.

He smiled, "This should help," he said. "This will help. A lot."

He stood, she remained seated and they both just stared at the pile of money.

In the blink of an eye, their debts were gone, their refrigerator and food pantry were bursting and they were able to pack up their car and take a vacation. While they were not well off, for the first time since Joe got off that boat all those years ago, he had some breathing room.

Chapter 13

We got off the elevator on the second floor and walked down a long hallway. Maura hit a large, metallic button mounted waist-high on the right hand wall that automatically opened two doors to the critical care unit. The hospital was nice but it was cold and sterile…you know, a hospital.

I slowed my pace a bit, falling to the rear of our four-person pack headed down to the end of the hallway. Dad was in the corner room, right next to the nurses' station.

Maura walked in first and joyfully exclaimed, "Look who's here!"

I still wasn't in the room. Steve entered then Jim. Mom had already come around the bed to greet each of us with a hug and kiss. She looked amazing for a woman who would be 91 in a matter of weeks; however, she had lost a lot of weight over the last six months. These challenges with Dad had taken a toll on her.

Jim approached Dad next as I silently waited in the back. When it was my turn, I shook his hand and repeated what each of my brother's had greeted him with, a simple, "Hi Dad."

Not exactly eloquent. I wasn't sure if anyone else had been contemplating this moment as much as I had but it worked for them so I was staying the course.

Dad responded the same to each of us. He kept saying, "I'm okay. I'm okay." He looked me clear in the eyes and raised both of his hands up by his shoulders, like a blackjack dealer showing their hands as they enter or leave a table. "I'm okay."

"I know," I said with a small smile and a reassuring nod.

Not only did I not "know" that but I did not think that either. What I knew, at this moment, was that he did not look okay. He looked weak and disconnected. His body slumped slightly to the right and he was gaunt. His hands fidgeted with Kleenex and the robe that the hospital assigned him continued to slip from his left shoulder. His eyes looked sore, watery and red.

"I'm okay." He repeated.

"I know," I repeated.

I had the closest proximity to Dad but, initially, said the least. For us, it was good to go in as a group - especially as a loud, raucous Irish group always wanting to have a good time. As Jim and Steve peppered Dad with questions, I got to stand back a bit and take it all in.

In retrospect, being a casual observer may not have been the best situation for me. While I was hearing the conversation, my mind couldn't overcome the questions of how many conversations would there be left to hear. As much as I would tell myself to stay in the moment, those thoughts of an end would not relent.

I walked down to the foot of the bed leaving a space open for Steve to move closer. I began speaking to Mom, as Dad was doing far more listening than speaking. He broke from the conversation and looked around the room.

"I thought I died and went to Heaven this morning," Dad said, his speech coming soft and low. "I thought I died."

"Why did you think that, Dad?" Steve asked.

Dad's head turned and glanced at each of us. "Because of all of you coming down."

Mom gave a small laugh, slowly shook her head, smiled and said, "Gerard, you're fine."

I looked at Mom, Maura, Jim and Steve and then turned to Dad and said, "Dad, you really think *this* is Heaven?"

Jim then commented under his breath, "If this is Heaven, I'd hate to see what you would end up getting in the other place."

It was time for Dad to have dinner and Mom had to handle a couple of things with the on-duty nurse. She asked that we "go run down to the cafeteria."

My parents never ask for help; they only ask that you get out of the way when something needs to be handled. We knew she had something personal to discuss with the nurses so we disappeared down to the cafeteria for a bite to eat.

Chapter 14

When Japan bombed Pearl Harbor, Dad immediately announced that he was enlisting in the Marines. The trouble was, Dad was 16 and his father refused to sign the papers. Standing in their living room, Dad pleaded his case.

There was an attack on our soil, people were dying and the world was in grave danger. None of these realities were lost on Joseph. However, there was no way Dad, at the time, could comprehend the feeling of a parent staring at a young child volunteering to put themselves in a situation in which survival was not only not guaranteed, it was also not a good wager.

"Not now," was all Joseph would say. "You're too young."

"You came here alone on a boat when you were 12," Dad argued, his voice elevating.

"No one was shooting at me," Joseph calmly replied.

Irish stubbornness dug its heels in on both sides. They were also both smart enough to know they each held losing hands. Dad was too young; he couldn't go until his father signed the papers. Joseph knew that as soon as his son reached the legal age, he was gone. They brokered a deal. Joseph said, "If you still want to go when you are 17, I won't stand in your way."

"You'll sign the papers?" Dad asked.

"On one condition," Joseph replied.

Dad's teeth clenched. In his mind he had already given his one concession of waiting until he was 17. "What's the condition?" he asked warily.

"I expect that you will complete high school first, and then I'll sign." Joseph had not completed his education and he wanted to see his son earn his degree.

Dad was all set to argue that there would be time to finish his degree upon his return and that the military needed him a lot more than St. Charles. But before those words flowed from his mouth he realized that his graduation would be approximately the same time that he turned 17. It actually made sense.

Getting through school was a challenge. Dad was never an ambitious student and, to make matters worse, felt that he shouldn't be there now. He should be overseas helping win this War.

His desire to serve his country never wavered. Mom and Dad had three friends who were killed in the attack on Pearl Harbor and a number of others who lost their lives in battle already. Two of Mom's brothers, Jim and Joe, had already enlisted in the Army. Dad anxiously awaited graduation day.

Mom, being a year ahead of Dad in school, had already graduated and was working full time at the Waltham Horological Company, pulling in $18 per week. When the War began, Raytheon needed the company to switch their focus to making parts for planes. Mom's pay immediately increased to $42 per week. Upon receiving her first paycheck she went directly to Clarkson's Furniture and bought her mother a dining room set.

Dad committed to go into the United States Marine Corps in January of 1943; he would graduate in June. The recruitment office agreed that he would be allowed to graduate but, they cautioned, when called he had to be ready to leave within 24 hours. He said he understood.

Two weeks after graduation, Dad was driving down the street in the McShane Oil truck and Pearl Mahony, one of his friends, was standing on the side of the road frantically waving her arms and calling his name.

"What's the matter Pearl?" Dad asked. "Are you alright?"

"Am I alright?" Pearl repeated. "Yes, I'm fine. But, Gerard, a letter was just delivered to your house from the Marines. You leave tomorrow morning at 6:00 a.m.!"

Dad sat dumbfounded for a moment. Not that he wasn't anxious to serve but he couldn't believe that he was getting pulled that quickly without warning (even though he later did realize that they warned him that could happen).

"That can't be right Pearl," Dad said. "They'd give me more time than that."

"I'm telling you, Gerard, that's what it said."

"I'm going to go see," Dad said as he put the truck into gear and began to pull back out into the street.

"Good luck, Gerard," she called to him.

He glanced in her direction still unsure if she had the story straight and drove directly to his house. His mother was standing by the kitchen table where the letter was resting. He picked it up and read in silence. Pearl was right.

"Looks like I'm headed to Paris Island at 6:00 a.m. tomorrow."

Chapter 15

Upon returning from the cafeteria, we found Dad to be engaged and alert.

He gave a half smile when we reentered the room. "They're back," he softly said as a greeting.

On occasion he would speak but, mostly, he was an active listener. He would have moments where he would drift off to sleep but would come back and flow into the conversation. He would actually come back to drive the conversation to what he wanted to know.

Each kid had their topics, mine were pretty standard.

"How is Jillian (my oldest daughter) doing at UMass?"

"Really well. She is enjoying her classes and getting acclimated to being in college."

"Which one is she at?" He asked, his eyes slightly fluttering from exhaustion.

"Which one? Uh, Isenberg. The business school."

He looked confused, "Is that Amherst?"

"Oh, yeah," I said. "She is at UMass, Amherst."

I liked this. All normal, routine, boring. Just what I was hoping for. No Hallmark-life's-most-precious-moments stuff yet. No one trying to talk about how these are the important times that we must cherish. Just simple, mundane conversation.

"How about Kathleen (my middle daughter), what's she doing now?"

"She's a junior in high school. Doing very well. Looking at colleges."

"Which ones?"

"Well, a bunch actually…but I think her top two are UMass and American University in DC."

"You would probably save some money if she went with UMass," he said.

Even better than boring. Frugal. Perfect. Now the conversation really felt natural.

"Yeah," I responded. "you got that right."

"And Caroline?"

"She's in 8th grade. Everything is going just fine for her. Starting defense on the soccer team. She has a big leg, packs some power in the kicks."

He nodded. "Good, good," he said softly as he closed his eyes and drifted back off into a light sleep.

Jim, Steve, Maura, Mom and I continued talking about our trip as he slept in the bed positioned in the middle of us. Each time our conversation stalled you could hear the deep breaths he was taking in through his nose. On occasion one of us would adjust his blankets which would become bunched with every shift or slouch of his body weight.

Steve mentioned the light traffic on the drive from the airport. That statement triggered an immediate response from Dad.

"I miss driving," Dad exclaimed. " I should have never sold my Hyundai."

Dad bought his Hyunda new in 2004 and he loved that automobile. Over the next 12 years he put 31,812 (in total) miles on that car. When it was time that he needed to stop driving he worked out a deal to sell the car to a local garage for $4,000. I found out about the deal after the transaction was already agreed upon.

When a complication with the sale occurred I jumped in and said that I would give them the $4,000 for the car. Mom and Dad did not want to take my money but they also knew that it wasn't fair to the other kids to just give me the car. I was thrilled. The car was in new condition and we desperately needed a third vehicle now that we had four licensed drivers in the house.

"Well, I'm happy you decided to sell it," I said.

"Gerard, remember Patrick bought that car," Mom added.

He was confused at first but then remembered that I did buy the Hyundai from them.

"How's it driving?" he asked.

"Perfect," I reassured him. "It's great. I'm the primary driver; it's getting more use now than ever."

"How many miles have you put on it?" he asked.

"About 4,000," I responded.

His eyes opened wide.

"4,000?" he repeated.

"Yes," I said. "I have had it for a couple of months."

"Hmmmm," he said softly. "I guess that's about right. I used to put 25,000 miles a year on cars."

Steve walked up behind me and softly said, "I don't think he's too happy with that answer."

After more small talk I said to Dad that Jim told me something at the airport that I never knew, that he did not partner with my grandfather on McShane Oil when he was 19 but he purchased half the business and they ran two separate McShane Oil companies. Both of my parents immediately confirmed that was the case.

"Yes, Gerard wanted to run his own company," Mom said.

"My Father was very set in his ways," Dad explained. "He wanted to eat every day at 8:00 a.m., noon and 5:00 p.m. So, if we were busy, we would stop, go home, eat and then head back out for the night. I didn't want any part of that. I liked to work straight through and get home. I knew it was not going to work out so we felt it would be best to separate the businesses."

"We took range oil and Grandpa took heating oil," Mom explained.

"How much did you buy half the business for, Dad?" Steve asked.

"$5,000," Dad said. "That was tough to come by in 1944."

"It's not easy to come by in 2016 either," Steve replied.

Chapter 16

Following his graduation from boot camp, Dad was deployed to Guam.

For those who may be interested in war stories and tales of heroism, you're going to have to stream *Saving Private Ryan*. Dad didn't talk about war or his accomplishments. Any questions about it were met with dismissive statements like he did nothing different than what everyone else at the time was doing. His opinion was that there was nothing special to discuss.

Someone once said to me the people who talk the most about their military service are usually the people who never really saw the true horrors of war. Dad was in the middle of the horrors. Nightmares could not hold a candle to the terror these men experienced and when it was over they did all they could to bury it away deep inside of them. Not wanting to personalize or think about those that they opposed. The only way to move forward was to understand that they represented good and the other side represented evil. Good needed to prevail and it was their responsibility.

While Dad never talked about times of war, others did talk about his service and heroism. While the stories are not abundant because of his modesty, the general consensus was that he was not immune to fear but his faith and courage made him believe that life had more of a purpose for him. Some felt that his belief that he would always make it through the War and come back home emboldened Dad, more than most, to put himself in harm's way for the benefit of others.

In one battle, a member of Dad's platoon was struck by shrapnel throughout his torso and face, he was immediately blinded. In shock, he wandered aimlessly behind enemy lines as the combat raged. Dad was safe in a bunker, and watched with dreadfulness as his friend began drifting further into danger. Dad propped himself up on one knee. He arched his back. Just a few months earlier he was in this same position running track at St. Charles. He just needed to get to his friend and he was confident he could get him back safely.

The sergeant crouched in cover near Dad. He saw Dad's body shifting and knew what he was thinking. As bullets whizzed by their bunker, the sergeant screamed, "Stay down Mac, don't even think about it!"

The end of the sentence hadn't escaped the sergeant's lips when Dad broke into a full speed run through the bullets and mortar fire. He began calling to his friend as he raced towards him. Dad scooped him up, threw him over his shoulder and raced back to safety. Under the cover of protective fire from their troops, both my father and his friend made it back behind bunkers without further injury. His friend lost his vision but ended up leading a successful life in New York as the owner and operator of a candy store.

While the War was raging overseas, life continued back home and Dad always wanted to ensure that he was keeping everything on track. He managed to save $350 that he sent home to Mom to go out and buy herself an engagement ring. This is about the peak of Irish romance. Mom didn't know what she was looking for but her boss invested in jewelry so she gave him the money to buy her a nice ring. Her boss traveled in to the Jeweler's Building in Boston and bought her a beautiful engagement ring.

Dad's cousin went into the jewelry business years later and took a look at Mom's ring and said that it was a perfect stone. When he was told that they purchased it for $350, he laughed and said there was no way that stone ever sold for $350. It wasn't until that moment that Mom and Dad realized that her boss had also contributed a significant sum of his own money to ensure she had the perfect ring.

Three months after Mom received her ring, Dad was crouched in a foxhole with enemy fire exploding all around him. He and Sergeant Hainge were returning fire but were under a relentless attack. A mortar shell exploded near them, filling Dad with shrapnel. He felt a sharp pain and blacked out.

He awoke on a boat, heading for a hospital. His recuperation time in hospitals ended up taking a full year, first in the South Pacific, then in Washington and, finally, in Boston at the Chelsea Naval Hospital. He was awarded a Purple Heart.

Over 70 years later, as Dad was confined to his bed in a skilled nursing facility, my brother Mike was talking to him about the internet and how easy it is to research people from the old days.

"Anyone you want to look up?" Mike asked Dad.

After a few moments of thinking Dad said, "Haingey. I would love to know what happened and how I got on that boat. I'm sure he saved my life, I just can't figure out how he did it."

Mike searched old military databases and could not come up with any information. He tried multiple sites, including a listing of World War II veterans but still, nothing.

Months passed and Mike received an email from a Mr. Dick Hainge, he said that he was contacted by someone who noticed search activity on one of the World War II veteran's sites of someone looking up his father. He asked if he could help.

Mike relayed the story and Dick Hainge said his father just passed two months prior, a month after my brother began his search. Mr. Hainge said that he was aware of some details of the story and that his father did have a hand in getting Dad to safety. He said that he would be in Clearwater, Florida the following week and asked if my brother would like to meet.

Mike enthusiastically said yes. Unfortunately, Mike's wife Ann had a bad fall and needed immediate medical attention. Communication between

Mike and Mr. Hainge broke down. The email my brother was contacting him on was no longer working and all discussions ended.

While we never learned the story of how Dad's life was saved, we are all indebted forever to Haingey.

Chapter 17

We all remained standing around Dad's bedside. Same stories and conversation as we had time and time again but now we clung to them like pieces of gold.

It's like water. You don't give water a second thought when you are going to the sink to fill up a glass but if you're out in the heat, and you know there is only a limited supply, you think about it, crave it, savor it and pray that more appears.

"What did you do in the summer months when you owned the oil company," I asked.

"Nothing," he responded.

"You mean the work was slow," I said.

"No," he said. "I mean nothing. But during the winter months I could work upwards of 120 hours each week. A call comes in at 2:00 a.m. from someone who doesn't have heat - what are you going to do call one of your guys? I'd just go and handle it myself."

As we talked about the past his spirits rose; his whole demeanor changed. The focus was off his condition and became more on his (and our) life. He still was not as active of a conversationalist as he was six months ago. However, he was sitting up straight. He laughed and joked.

After another hour of casual conversation he nestled back down into the hospital bed, slouching significantly to the right. This time he did not look sickly, just exhausted. He shut his eyes but continued to listen to the conversation. He would grin slightly at a funny comment and his head would turn ever so slightly if the conversation became serious.

There was a momentary pause, and Dad's voice broke the stillness. It was said with a sense of wonderment and urgency. A topic that was, and always had been, of paramount importance in our home.

"How are the Sox doing?" he asked with closed eyes.

"They're in first place," I said, lying. "Half game in front of Baltimore." In actuality they were in second place, a half game behind Baltimore but if this was ever his last night on Earth, I wanted him to go out thinking the Red Sox were in first place.

He opened his eyes, "Good," he said with a smile.

"And the Yankees are in last place," I added.

"Good," he repeated and his smile grew bigger as he closed his eyes once again.

I couldn't resist getting under his skin, "You know Dad, some people up in Boston are saying that Big Papi (David Ortiz) might just be the best Red Sox player of all time."

With his eyes still shut he shook his head, he then opened his eyes, looked directly at me and said one word, "Williams."

It was 7:45 p.m. and time for us to go. We said our good-byes and made our way to the door. As we exited, we each paused and glanced back, capturing the moment, silently praying that there would be more.

We were heading out for a bite to eat and to pick up some groceries for home. Maura had turned her house into a barracks for us and we needed to get settled.

Chapter 18

Dad was told that he would be granted a 30-day leave from the Chelsea Naval Hospital.

"That's when we should get married," Dad said to Mom.

She agreed.

When Mom went home and told her Mother the plan she simply said, "You're crazy." When Dad's parents visited the hospital and he told them the plan they said, "What are you doing? You're rushing everything. There's plenty of time for that."

When they approached Father Kenney they got the response for which they were looking. He leaned back, smiled and said, "I have to tell you, I've been wondering what's been taking the two of you so long." They were 19.

Father Kenney married them on Tuesday, January 9, 1945 at St. Charles Church. Joseph requested a June wedding because he was too busy in the winter months with the oil business. They declined the June wedding recommendation but looked for a solution that would best satisfy all parties.

"What's your slowest day of the week?" Dad asked his father. "Still Tuesdays?"

"Yes," his father responded. "I suppose."

"Here's what we'll do, we'll get married in January, like we want but we'll get married on a Tuesday to work best with your schedule." Neither was going to get a full win so they agreed on each receiving a partial victory.

When my parents contacted St. Charles with the odd request for a Tuesday wedding, they were met with enthusiasm. Ultimately, the administration contacted them and said that not only were they fine with a Tuesday wedding but they were going to allow the Juniors and Seniors to take a day off if they wished to attend the ceremony.

Mom and Dad were thrilled. Their reception was a bit smaller, held at the Log Cabin Restaurant on Moody Street in Waltham. They honeymooned in New York, which is the furthest west Mom ever ended up traveling in her lifetime.

Dad's parents offered Mom and Dad $1,500 cash or $1,500 as a down-payment on a house for their wedding present. They were very tempted to take the cash because they had nothing. After thinking it through, though, they took the gift as a down-payment for a house that cost $5,200.

"It might have been the smartest move I ever made," Dad said. "If we had taken the cash we might have just blown it on a car and become renters. This got us off to a good start."

The local paper wrote that *after their honeymoon Florence Vallely would be returning home to live with her mother at 63 Taylor Street while Gerard McShane would go to Chelsea Naval Hospital.* Mom said it sounded like she was going to beat him up.

Following their honeymoon, Mom was visiting Dad in the hospital when the announcement was made that the war was over. The hospital administration went into complete lockdown and said that all busses and trains had been cancelled and that the revelry was causing some areas to be dangerous.

Dad went to the head of administration and said someone had to get Mom home safely.

"We can't have her walk home with all this going on," he pleaded. "People are out of control out there."

"I don't know what we can do," the administrator said in a giddy state. "People are just celebrating."

"I get it," Dad said. "But that celebrating is out of control. Just do me a favor and find someone who will just give her a lift back to her house."

The administrator saw the concern and seriousness in Dad's eyes. "You have my word, she will get home safe."

Twenty minutes later, the administrator came back and said, "We have a car waiting to take you home." He escorted Mom downstairs where the Admiral's car was waiting. The driver pulled up to the front entrance, got out and walked around the car and opened the door.

He greeted her with, "Ma'am," as she stepped into the vehicle. The car door closed behind her and she was driven through the throngs of celebrants and back to her home on Taylor Street.

A few months later, Dad was finally released from the time he spent in hospitals. After seeing his immediate family he made a beeline to Candyland. The thought of Boris' ice cream never ceased to draw him.

As always a line stretched all the way from the counter to the door and Dad waited silently, bemused by Boris' ability to keep an entire shop quiet with just the threat of taking away their ability to order his food.

In the midst of the chaos, Boris glanced up toward the end of the line, stopped and walked out from behind the counter. Everyone including Dad stood silently watching and wondering what he was doing or, more likely, if someone in line had done something that was going to get them kicked out of the shop.

Boris walked directly to Dad and extended his hand. Dad was a bit dumbfounded as he reached out and grasped Boris' hand in a shake. "Welcome home, Mr. McShane," Boris said. Dad nodded and murmured, "Thank you." He was thrown by this encounter.

In all the years of going to Candyland, he was always just a face in the crowd and never had any significant interaction with Boris. He didn't expect Boris to recognize him after all this time, let alone know his name.

Boris did not even take his order; he just went back around the counter, tightly packed two quarts of ice cream and put them on the counter next to two pounds of chocolate. Boris said, "Thank you for your service, Mr. McShane." Dad tried to pay but Boris shook his head and repeated, "Thank you for your service."

Dad was always embarrassed by recognition for serving in the military. It was his belief that it was his duty and responsibility and not something that was done for thanks or reward.

Chapter 19

Maura lives in a nice three bedroom ranch with a two car garage, two full bathrooms and a very large screened patio that houses the bar, a small pool table and different areas of seating. It's an ideal location for get-togethers and a perfect sized home for Maura, her boyfriend Tim, her daughter Jacquelyn, and Tim's son Thomas.

And then, for a week, you add me, Jim and Steve and we were large, loud and spread out all over their comfortable abode. Steve was assigned to Thomas' room, Thomas was reassigned to the master bedroom with Maura and Tim, Jim had a blowup queen-sized mattress placed in a small open space in between Jacquelyn's room and Thomas' room; and they removed their dining room table and put a bed in that space for me.

The day was emotional and exhausting, now was the perfect time to collapse into chairs and the couch to watch the NBA playoffs. The coffee table was covered with food and the conversation would randomly jump from one nonsensical subject to another.

We purposefully avoided deep conversations.

After a couple of hours we said our goodnights and headed to our designated sleeping areas, well aware that our aging, weak bladders would probably have us bumping into each other again well before morning.

I pray every night. Not in the traditional sense of kneeling beside your bed and reciting an Our Father or Hail Mary. My prayer is most often a conversation, and occasionally an argument.

Most of my discussions with God start with, "Hey God." I'm not sure why I feel that I can be so informal with The Creator but I figure He had a hand in making me so He probably shouldn't be too shocked at my tremendous level of informality. I usually continue, "I'm having a hard time understanding something. If you want me…"

In a nutshell, there it is: I try to push my problems on to God saying that He put me in this position for a reason and I'm pointing out that there is something abundantly unfair about the position. So, without directly asking, I guess I do hope that God says to Himself, "You know, Patrick's got a point. I never considered that angle."

I almost never pray for myself but I do tend to pray for people that have to deal with me on a regular basis. I ask for visions of where I am supposed to be and what I am supposed to be doing. Like many, I have challenges finding meaning in my life; however, I do see great meaning in the three lives that my wife and I created.

Sometimes I ask if this whole afterlife belief is real. If it's not real, I'm not sure who I am asking. If it is real, I may get in trouble for the question. Kind of a lose/lose proposition. Sometimes it seems too convenient. Everyone will be happy and back together and the greatest joy you have ever had on Earth will not come close to matching your least great experience in Heaven. And, by the way, this is for eternity. Eternity. A lot of times I can find myself thinking that it's all a big, beautiful work of fiction that keeps us from going insane from thinking that this life is all we have. That when lives end; we won't get to see these people ever again or hear their voices or share a laugh.

But here's the thing, I keep talking to God.

Every day in every situation, I keep talking. While I don't believe that God reaches down and places His hand on my head and turns me to the right direction, I also can look back and say, "How did we make it this far?" Through some tremendous financial and emotional challenges, somehow we persevere. There have been years where our bank account reminds me of the story of the fishes and the loaves. There certainly wasn't enough in there to get through some challenges that we had to overcome but we did and there was still a little bit left at the end. Still standing, far stronger than I ever imagined.

I want proof, we all want proof. That's why so many buy the books and go to private meetings with the hustlers who claim to be able to "speak with the dead." We all want a glimpse to say, okay, I saw a picture of the Pearly Gates and they are really pearly so it's all legit. But we don't get that glimpse. We get Faith, which is supposed to be better than proof…but a picture would be nice.

As I lay in bed that night, the light of the moon poured in through the window on the front door of Maura's house and illuminated much of the dining and living room areas. I thought back to a conversation I had with Mom a number of years prior.

Mom had called me to tell me that her sister Rita died. Her voice wavered but never broke. She would never allow a child to see or hear her in a weakened state. She took a deep breath and began to tell me about a dream she had just hours before. Mom had never, to the best of my recollection, told me of a dream.

In the dream, she said that she and Dad were sitting in the bleachers at St. Charles High School and Rita was proudly marching down the track leading throngs of children marching behind her. At that time, Rita was living in a skilled nursing facility. Rita motioned to Mom and Dad to come down and join her with a big smile on her face and a wave of her arm.

Mom and Dad jumped from their place in the bleachers and rushed down into the throngs of children and followed Rita. The group marched along the track and then out onto the field where they finally ended up at a stone wall. Rita climbed up on the stone wall and looked back at Mom and Dad and said, "Come on up!"

Mom lifted her leg to get up on the wall but the wall grew in height at just that moment and she was unsuccessful. Rita motioned again and Mom said that, in the dream, she looked at Dad and he tried to help her up on the wall but the wall grew once more. Rita looked down at them and smiled. She then turned, stepped off the wall and started walking, step after step up into the air as my parents and the children watched in awe. Eventually she disappeared into the clouds.

With a jerk of her head, Mom woke and was shaken from the dream. As with any dream that feels a bit too real she tossed for a while in her bed before embracing the fact that her sleep was officially done for the evening. She got out of bed, put on her robe and made her way to the kitchen to make some coffee and read a little. When my Father awoke she told him in detail about the dream. A short while after finishing the story, the phone rang.

It was then that she was given the news that Rita died early that morning.

After pausing a couple of times, me knowing but never acknowledging that she was taking the phone away from her face to compose herself, I could hear her take a deep breath. Then with a very controlled, slow and steady tone she said, "But like I said to your Father, thank God we didn't get up on that wall."

Here I was, laying in bed, in my sister's dining room in Florida. Dad was actively passing; I was thinking about my Aunt who had died years earlier. And I was smiling. Truthfully, I was almost laughing. I was feeling joy on two fronts, the first is that I loved that my family refused to let go of their sense of humor even (especially) in the most painful of all situations. The second was that even though I know we are not supposed to be looking for proof, it is nice to get glimpses once in a while that there is something bigger that we cannot comprehend. There is some connectivity between us that cannot be explained. Nothing ever drives that feeling home in me more than that dream that awoke Mom at just about the same moment her sister was passing from this Earth.

My prayer was simple. It was for Dad to be comfortable, for Mom to have strength during these impossible times. I also prayed for Dad to stick around and be engaged and involved when my sister Joyce and her husband Mike arrived tomorrow so they could be given the same gift of his presence as we were given today.

"Hey God," I simply instructed, "give us another day."

Chapter 20

Eight of us - Mike, Jim, Marsha, Ed, Steve, Joyce, Patrick and Maura - call Florence and Gerard McShane Mom and Dad. My parents started having children at 21 years old and didn't call it quits until they were 43. While having a kid every 2.7 years sounds overwhelming, in actuality, it was a bit crazier. The first six kids were born in the first 11 years. I came ten years after that (surprise) and Maura was born (most likely to keep me busy) a few years after me.

When Maura was in her 40s she was sitting with Mom at their dining room table, a round, glass topped structure with light colored wood sides. Sun shone in through the window and the conversation was light and whimsical. Seeing an opening, Maura asked the question to which most assumed that they knew the answer.

"In all seriousness," Maura said directly confronting Mom with a sneak attack, "was Patrick a mistake?"

Mom shook her head and said, "Maura!" She got up and walked into the kitchen. "What kind of a question is that?"

Maura said, "Come on, I won't tell, I just want to know. Was he a mistake?"

Mom walked back to the table, sat down and said, "You really want to know?"

Maura emphatically responded, "Yes!"

Mom replied, "All eight of you were mistakes."

The widespread distribution of kid's ages resulted in births taking place in four different decades, the 40s, 50s, 60s and 70s. In 1979 I was given The Guinness Book of World Records as a birthday present. Bad timing. As much as I looked I could not see a record of someone having kids in five different decades. I implored my mother to have a kid in 1980 as it was our ticket to the record books. She informed me that this was not going to happen.

"Patrick, I'm going to be 55 in 1980. You keep looking at another way you can get into the record book. I'm all set." To this day I have never met another person who had kids in four different decades, let alone five. We would have made Guinness.

Mom and Dad had their first child, Mike, two years into their marriage. The day he was born, Dad briskly walked down Moody Street to visit Mom in the hospital. Dad waited patiently (nervously) until he was finally called in to see her.

Mom was out of it, gassed on ether and just lying there. Dad stood in the room with nurses standing all around him smiling. He smiled back. They all looked at him nodding and smiling. He nodded and smiled.

Finally after about a minute that seemed like an hour he raised his hands to shoulder height, palms facing the ceiling and said, "What am I supposed to do?"

One of them said, "Kiss her."

And he did.

With the birth of Mike, and a couple of the other kids, my parents would need to sell the family car to pay the hospital bill. Money wasn't tight in those days, it was non-existent.

Dad refused to drive the McShane Oil truck to go places; he considered that to be for work use only. He would walk until he saved up enough money to buy another vehicle. If he had taken the work truck, he felt that he would be creating a solution that would make his life easier but adversely affect his business asset. Forcing himself to walk created an uncomfortable solution that he was focused on solving.

The production line kept pumping out those kids and cars kept getting sold to pay for hospital bills. There was also the constant shifting of kids to homes for care when Mom went into the hospital. We are talking the 1940s and 1950s for the birth of the first six kids. While Dad could do a lot, he was not a primary caregiver.

When Jim was born, my parents brought Mike to Nana's, my mother's mother. When Marsha was born, my parents brought Mike and Jim to Nana's. By the time Ed, Steve and Joyce were born, the older kids would be sent to Grammy's, my father's mother, and the younger ones to Nana's.

While Grammy was a wonderful person who would load you up on Hoodsies (vanilla and chocolate ice cream in a little paper cup with a pull off top and a wooden spoon), she was not a gourmet. One of the staple sandwiches that she made for Mike and Jim to bring to school was butter and jelly. Not peanut butter and jelly. Butter and jelly. No one was sure where this butter and jelly combination originated from, probably a misunderstanding, but she continued to believe that they loved this sandwich and they didn't have the heart to tell her that they spent much of their school lunch period methodically scraping off butter.

With the birth of each child, Mom and Dad would move in to Nana's house for a week. This was the more desired location. Nana was a really good cook and she did a great job caring for Mom while Dad was working.

Any of the kids would tell you, thank God for the support system that was in place because if it was up to Dad, there may have never been a diaper that got changed.

Chapter 21

Jim, Steve and I picked up Mom and drove to the hospital a little after 10 a.m. that next morning. Maura was able to go back to work for a day since we were all in town. She had taken a lot of time off to be in the hospital over the last couple of weeks.

From a health standpoint, Dad was somewhere between where he was when we first walked in yesterday and where he ended up last night. He was feeling pretty good and looked okay for his age and situation. He was a follower of the conversation but not much of an active participant.

Jim sat on a chair against the wall on the far side of the room. Steve and I were speaking with Dad on the left hand side of the bed while Mom attended to his various needs while leaning in from the right hand side of the bed.

She made sure he was comfortable and acted as a 94-pound protector against anything that could go wrong. This was not a new responsibility, she always looked out for him and he looked out for her.

Dad glanced past Mom for a second and looked in Jim's direction.

"What's that?" he asked.

Mom looked behind her and turned back with a confused look on her face. "That's Jim," she responded.

"No, around Jim's head," Dad continued. "What's that light?"

We all looked towards the dull white color of the wall with no light emanating from anywhere.

"What are you talking about, Gerard?" Mom asked. "There's no light."

Steve said, "It's Jim, Dad probably sees a halo." It has been a long-standing joke in our family that Jim has always been the favorite. This started back in the late 1960s when Jim joined the Marine Corps to serve in Vietnam. He fought in the thick of very serious battles and returned home with two Purple Hearts. Ever since then, all the siblings would try to give Mom and Jim a hard time about the favoritism. Jim embraced the role. Mom always laughed…but never denied.

Jim responded, "It's alright, Dad. Mom's been seeing a halo around my head since the day I was born."

We all laughed but, every once in a while, Dad would glance back over in that direction.

"Dad," Steve said, "Patrick and I are going to get Joyce and Mike."

"Good," he said. "That's good."

As I left the room, Jim was asking Dad about one of his business partners. I had a fear of missing out as I just wanted to capture every conversation and drink them in and save them for a lifetime.

Chapter 22

Mom and Dad were never impressed by a person because of the size of their bank account. It really was never even a topic of conversation. Oh, there were times where they would say, "Did you see their home?" or "Their new car would probably cost me a year's pay."

They never held someone's wealth against them; it was just not something that impressed them. The character of an individual would be a regular topic of conversation. We had neighbors that were worth tens of millions of dollars, however, the only story I remember Dad talking about was when their ten year-old son was walking past our house on the way to the bus stop and he trudged through snow that went up to his thigh, to lay my parent's Boston Globe on our front step. "He didn't ring the bell, he didn't look for recognition," Dad would say, "he just helped us out and didn't need for us to know who did it. That's how you know a family is raising their kids right."

While Mom and Dad would always welcome a financial opportunity, they would never take a nickel they didn't earn.

Dad strolled into the local bank on Main Street in Waltham to break a $100 bill. This was in the late 1950s and it was fairly common for Dad to be making this transaction as a lot of his oil customers paid in person by cash.

"Good morning, Gerard," he was greeted by the teller. There were no other customers in front of him.

He smiled and nodded. "Good morning. Can I get two tens, ten fives and thirty ones."

The bank manager came over and joked a bit with Dad and the teller was joining in as he counted out the money into a clean stack. Dad glanced around as the manager pointed out various renovations being done. When he turned back the teller was smiling at him and his stack of bills sat neatly in the center of the counter with a $10 bill resting on the top.

Dad was in a rush and could tell that he was going to get swept up into another conversation, so he scooped the stack of bills off the counter saying, "I've got to run."

He stepped up and into the oil truck and rifled through the bills to ensure the count was correct and to make sure each bill was facing front and that the presidents were all upright and not flipped upside down. Dad did not like upside down presidents in his stacks of currency.

He quickly realized that the teller made a mistake. Dad went back into the bank to the teller that assisted him and said, "You're a little off on the count today."

The teller looked pained, "Gerard," he said, "I know you're honest. We all know you're honest but as soon as a customer leaves the window, the transaction is done. There are no exceptions."

"But your count is off," Dad said. "I gave you a $100 and this is the stack you gave me," Dad said putting the stack down on the table back in front of the teller with the $10 resting on top."

"I understand and I would never say you tampered with the stack but you have to understand that the moment you leave the window the transaction is complete. If it was up to me, I'd fix it for you but its company policy we are not allowed to make an exception for anyone." The teller liked Dad and clearly was uncomfortable having this interaction.

Dad shrugged, "It's okay, I get it. If it's company policy it's company policy," Dad just shook his head. "It's my fault for not counting it at the window."

"I am so sorry, Gerard," the teller repeated. "I, we, all trust you implicitly and know you are an honest man."

"Policies are policies," Dad said as placed his right hand on top of the stack of bills the teller had given him and fanned them out across the teller's counter. There were two tens, ten fifties and thirty twenties. Dad asked one more time, "No exceptions?"

On that morning, the bank made an exception to their policy.

This was not Mom and Dad's only touch with a potential banking error, cash windfall. They were two of the great certificate of deposit hunters of their time. Being children of the depression, they were always cautious about the stock market. So their investments would bounce from one CD to another, always searching for an additional 1/8 or ¼ of a point somewhere.

One such time, they cashed in a $10,000 CD at a bank in Clearwater Florida to invest in another CD offered by a bank right down the street. They were laughing and joking with the representative from the bank as he was plugging their check into the computer for processing. He signed the check and wished them well knowing that they would be back for their next promotion.

Mom was holding the check as they were walking down the street. She glanced down and said, "Hey Gerard, looks like interest really piled up on this CD."

"What do you mean?" he said, glancing in her direction but not breaking stride.

As they walked, Mom stuck the check in front of his face. Instead of being for $10,000 plus accumulated interest, the amount on the check was for a little over $8 million. They stopped and just stared at this signed bank check made out in their names.

For a one-block walk they were wealthier than they had ever been, or would ever be.

They walked back into the bank and waited for the person who had just assisted them.

"We think you made a bit of a mistake on this check," Mom said.

The color quickly drained from his face, "I have no idea how that could have ever happened," he said. "Absolutely, no idea."

After reviewing everything he realized that he had punched their account number into the amount payable box.

Chapter 23

Traffic was heavy but moving on the way to the airport. Our Chevrolet rental had a V6 motor that was a bit sluggish. Each potential opening to make an advance in your current position was done with a bit of dread.

"Come on," Steve barked at the car. "You have to move when I hit the gas."

A few more tries later he smacked his right hand down on top of the steering wheel in obvious anguish. "This is nuts. This thing isn't going anywhere," he lamented. "Look at this idiot," he continued pointing out a little white Nissan Rogue that zipped in front of us. "You saw I was…" his voice trailed off.

And then his voice returned stronger than ever, "Idiot!"

I wasn't sure if that was meant for another car, driver, his car, himself or me. All in all, it was entertaining.

"What do you think about these hallucinations?" Steve asked diverting his attention from the war he was waging with every vehicle on the road, including his own.

"I don't know," I said. "Disconcerting, I guess."

"Yeah," he responded. "We probably shouldn't be too surprised just thinking about everything he's been going through."

"Yup," I said looking out at the rows of Publix supermarkets and Hess gas stations as we drove.

We then repeated all the same conversations that we have been having since yesterday morning when this journey began. I guess that's one of the benefits of being around people who are feeling the exact same things as you. There is no need for conversation; it's just experiencing the situation.

We swung into the arrival area of the airport and picked up Joyce and Mike. They were anxious, and peppered us with questions, mostly the same questions we had when we were heading in to see him yesterday. We were all thankful that Maura forwarded us a picture of him from a few days ago. It visually prepared us for his weakened state.

"So how far is it from here?" Joyce asked.

"Only a few minutes," Steve responded casually.

"Oh, that quick," she said. "Good. That's good." It wasn't good. No matter how much you prepare in these situations you always want some additional time to psyche yourself up. I noticed all the same trepidation in them that I had seen in myself yesterday.

We parked the car, walked across the large parking lot and opened the heavy, rectangular glass doors which led into the hospital lobby. Joyce had forced a grin on to her face as we stepped into the elevator. Mike stood in silence, wringing his hands with eyes focused on the floor. The elevator doors opened. Joyce looked at me and Steve and raised her eyebrows with a slight tilt of her head.

She wanted us to lead the way. She slowed her pace and fell to the back, looking down at the floor and towards the various notifications that lined the walls. Joyce shared a closed-lip grin with residents and employees as we passed. I could not help but notice a couple of deep breaths escape her mouth as we made our way down the hallway.

She had no idea that I was on to her, she was taking my move from yesterday.

Chapter 24

McShane Oil began with my grandfather, who also had a successful ice-distribution business in the summertime. When Grandpa realized the income generated from McShane Oil was sufficient to live on he just gave the ice distribution business away to a man who lived in the neighborhood who was looking to break away from his dead end job. Dad shook his head because he was sure that money was left on the table. Grandpa would just say that his knees and back didn't care about the money, they were just happy to not have to lug blocks of ice up flights and flights of stairs.

Dad bought and broke off half the oil business and when Grandpa had enough, Dad brought the two companies back together under the McShane Oil name.

The business grew to having nearly 400 customers handled by Dad and four contracted service employees. The contractors received $4 per visit plus any parts expenses that they incurred. There was a lot of trust in the company with most customers knowing Dad through St. Charles.

An important cog in the organization was Dad's assistant, Loretta. She had worked for a competing oil company and was proficient on an advanced adding machine. The other company was upgrading their technology and Dad saw an opportunity to grab a great employee.

He approached the owners of the business and asked if they might be interested in selling him their adding machine. They jumped at the chance to be compensated for something they were probably just going to send to the dump.

After he bought the machine, he reached out to Loretta and asked her if at this point in her career if she wished to learn all the new technology his competitor was implementing or if she would prefer to continue to work on equipment where she had a great comfort level. Loretta immediately took the opportunity to follow the adding machine with which she had such comfort and success. Dad then said that she could work from home and he had the adding machine set up at her house and a business phone line installed.

When other people saw technology, Dad saw people. He knew what motivated them. He knew that if he made Loretta's life easier for her and her family, his investment would pay off many times over. And it all happened while the competing company laughed at Dad for wanting dated technology. They didn't realize until the dust settled that Dad's aim was never the technology.

Dad worked hard at McShane Oil and knew it provided well for the family but he never liked his job. To be clear, he loathed his career. It wasn't mentally stimulating; he was either constantly working or caught in vast amounts of down time and knew he wanted a very different future for his children.

He loved real estate. He would spend hours driving around looking at homes and commercial property. Considerable chunks of every vacation were spent going to open houses and testing the market to see where a proper value on a home could be found.

In late 1958, my parents were contacted and offered a good sum of money to sell McShane Oil. They discussed that this just might be the break they were looking for so Dad could pursue his dream of working in real estate full time.

Mom and Dad sat on their living room sofa and made lists of pros and cons of venturing off into a new direction. They nearly convinced themselves that this was their destiny; they would sell the business, pack up the family and move to California. Dad would get into real estate sales and then, potentially, move into the development side of the business.

They kept talking, however, and scared themselves. The uncertainties were too much to consider. Was this the right time for such a drastic move? They had six kids, the oldest being 11, a successful business and all their family located within 15 miles of their home.

They passed and stayed in Waltham. Years later Dad would say that he, "was pre-determined to spend his life driving a truck for McShane Oil." That's half true - he was raised in the business and it was natural for him to go into the business. He was never going to leave the oil business, though not for lack of ability or drive. His family was growing and he was providing. For someone who was a gambler by nature, he took a very cautious approach to his career and that sealed his fate.

He never complained and always said that everything turned out great and he had no regrets.

Chapter 25

Joyce and Mike cautiously entered the hospital room, warmly greeted Dad and then each took a step backward. Almost unnoticeable but enough to give others in the room permission to take the lead in the conversation so they could adjust and take everything in…exactly like I had done 24 hours before.

Dad was not doing well, he was slumped heavily to the right. Attempts to prop his side up with a pillow would work for a small amount of time but then the pillow would give and his body would slowly start melting back into the sheets.

He wanted the bed to remain upright, he recognized Joyce and Mike and was happy about their arrival. He wanted to be seen as part of the group sitting upright and not viewed laying back in the hospital bed. However, he remained too tired to engage in a conversation.

After a while, Dad raised his right arm slightly and pointed to the ceiling and spoke of a door he just saw opening.

"The door is over here Gerard," Mom showed him, pulling the curtain back a bit. "You're pointing at the ceiling."

Dad glanced at the door and then his eyes drifted back up to the ceiling.

"You know what I bet you're seeing," Joyce added, "the rectangular light fixtures. They are the same shape as doors."

Dad's eyes looked at Joyce and then drifted to the actual door to the hallway. Then they went back up to the ceiling. "Probably," he said softly, his eyes remaining towards the sky.

Joyce gave Mom and Maura a break from the role of nurturer and actively began feeding him. She noticed that when he fed himself he would become discouraged and give up but if someone was keeping the food going towards his mouth he would continue to eat.

He was a shell of what he was the day before. He was weak, he could not get comfortable and was barely able to engage in conversation. He spoke in low murmurs and even those were only in response to questions he was being asked.

Dad wanted to be an observer of the conversations, not the centerpiece. So we talked. We talked about kids. We talked about trips. We talked about food. We talked about jobs. We talked about television shows. We talked about anything and everything.

In the middle of a conversation about where people were going to be eating dinner that night, Dad forcefully said, "Walcott took the hardest left I ever saw." He didn't move from how he was lying in his bed and his eyes never opened.

"Jersey Joe Walcott, Dad?" Jim said.

"Yes," Dad replied. "(Rocky) Marciano stepped right in and leveled him. Walcott went right to the mat." Dad's eyebrows raised slightly and he shook his head almost as if he was feeling the weight of Marciano's powerful left hand crashing down on the side of his head.

"Marciano was something else, huh Dad?" Jim said.

Dad nodded. "Next to (Joe) Louis, probably the best ever."

He wanted to be part of the conversation again. He was done being a spectator. His body was not cooperating but his mind was working.

Joyce moved closer to him on the left hand side of the bed. "Hey Dad," she said, "We just hit 200,000 miles on our Honda."

"How many?" he softly asked.

"200,000 miles."

"He's already put 4,000 miles on the Hyundai," Dad said motioning towards me. I guess Steve was right, that might have bothered him.

I was standing on the right hand side of the bed and had just pulled the hospital robe back up on his left shoulder. His continual slumping kept making the flimsy hospital gown slip. I went for the easy layup, the conversation he always loved having.

"Dad," I asked, "what year was your Cord?"

In the late 1940s, Dad owned a B12 convertible Cord. The Cord has been called the most recognizable American-made car ever made and it competed with the Dusenberg as the most beautiful car of the time. It is one of only a few automobiles to be displayed at the Museum of Modern Art in New York. Today, these automobiles can sell for hundreds of thousands of dollars.

"The best year ever," he said with directness, "1937."

"What color?"

"Yellow with a black top," he said. "It was beautiful."

Dad kept taking Kleenexes out of a box and folding them, when he was done folding he would either wipe his eyes or blow his nose. He would then discard that Kleenex and immediately grab another. On occasion he would grab his sheet, thinking it was the Kleenex.

"There was one time," he said, "I was the first car in line stopped at a red light on Moody Street and the first car that was stopped directly across from me on the other side was a Dusenberg. The people who got the green light didn't move. Everyone just stopped with their heads bouncing back and forth looking at these two cars."

"Did you ever see the car again after you traded it in?" I asked. In the late 40s he traded the Cord for a 1941 Buick. He said it was time to trade because parts were too hard to come by and he couldn't afford them when they could be found.

He gingerly began folding a new Kleenex, making sure that the sides lined up perfectly. He matched the corners and folded it in the center.

"No, never," he said in a voice only slightly higher than a whisper, his eyes transfixed on the Kleenex. "All my friends did, but I never saw it again."

He closed his eyes and changed the topic to the time and when dinner would be delivered.

"Do you want to try to get some sleep before dinner?" Mom asked.

"Probably," he said. Eyes shut.

"Why don't you guys go down for dinner," Mom said. "I'm going to stay here with him and maybe I'll meet you down there in a bit."

"I'll stay here too, Ma," Jim said.

Steve said that he would stay as well. I said I would take Joyce and Mike down and show them where the cafeteria was. Mom, Jim and Steve would meet us there after Dad fell asleep.

Chapter 26

Catholicism went without question in our household. Mom and Dad loved the time they spent in parochial school and found their foundation in faith to be of paramount importance as to how they raised their family and lived their lives.

Whenever Mom and Dad spoke of individuals who shaped their lives, their stories always centered on either their parents or various priests and nuns. When others would talk about how tough the nuns were in parochial school, they would silently shake their head.

"I'm not saying we never saw a kid get a wake-up call from a nun," Mom said. "But every one that I ever saw was well-deserved and none could be called a beating. More of a love-tap to keep them in line."

Dad laughed, "I took more than a couple pretty good shots. Those were no love taps…but I deserved them. In retrospect, I got off easy. You would think twice before stepping out of line, I'll tell you that much."

We weren't puritans or over the top with our religion. As a matter of fact, many would probably say we were skimming the surface. We did not say grace or regularly read the Bible. But attendance at Mass on Sunday morning or Saturday late afternoon was an absolute.

The only time a priest's order was not observed and obeyed from the alter was on a Sunday morning in 1950. When Mike was three years old he bolted from the pew one Sunday morning in the middle of Mass and made a beeline up and onto the altar at St. Charles.

As he ran my parents sat in terror because Mike had spent a great deal of time at Nana's house (Mom's mother) where Uncle Jim also lived. Big Jim was great but a tough guy. He dropped out of school after the sixth grade and worked as a grave digger. Big Jim had a very colorful vocabulary, of which, Mike had adopted some rather choice words that he exercised frequently.

Mom and Dad sat in the pew and watched Mike run-up on the altar where he laughed and ran around.

"Go get him," Dad said.

"No way," Mom replied. "You get him."

"I'm not budging," Dad replied as they sat and watched him run amok. "He learned those words from your brother, you get him."

As they continued to whisper their argument, the priest smiled and said, "May I ask who this child belongs to?"

Mom remained stoic, staring straight ahead at the altar. Dad sheepishly rose from the pew to collect his foul-mouthed son, who blessedly giggled and ran but did not utter a single curse.

My brother Ed's life was viewed by Mom and Dad as a direct result of divine intervention. Ed became gravely ill shortly after he was born and was having great pains in his effort to breathe. Mom called the hospital in a panic.

"Relax honey," the nurse on the phone said. "You are just being cautious because you have a new-born at home."

"This is my fourth," Mom tersely replied.

"Hang on," the nurse said with a decidedly different tone. "I'll contact Dr. Ryan immediately."

The nurse returned to the line a few minutes later. "Mrs. McShane, Dr. Ryan is leaving in 15 minutes and will come to your home."

Dr. Ryan was looking to get away for a long weekend and cutting out of work early to spend a weekend on the Cape. He could swing by the Newton house on the way.

Upon examination Dr Ryan said, "This boy needs to be admitted to the hospital now." He knew the situation was dire (it turned out to be bronchial pneumonia and a collapsed lung). Dr. Ryan stood in Mom and Dad's kitchen frantically dialing hospitals. Waltham first, they were at maximum capacity. Then another, maximum capacity, and another, maximum capacity. He then called Mount Auburn Hospital in Cambridge and they said they could take him. "He's on the way now," Dr. Ryan said.

Dr. Ryan left and Mom told Dad what to pack. She grabbed the phone and called the convent to have Sister Annatta pray for him.

"Florence," Sister Annatta said, "I have a religious relic that has never left my possession. Come to the convent before going to the hospital to put the relic on Ed. I feel it might save him." My parents were cautious because going to the convent would add fifteen minutes to getting Ed to the hospital. But they quickly surmised that this blessing was needed for his life to be saved.

Upon entering the hospital, Ed was immediately put in an incubator. A doctor came out to Mom and Dad and said that Ed had 24 hours to live. Mom and Dad went in to see Ed but did not see the relic.

"Where's the relic?" Mom asked.

"We can't put it on him in the…" a nurse responded.

"Put it on him," Mom said.

"I know this is hard but it's against the hospital policy to…" the nurse responded.

"We are his parents," Dad said. "Put the relic on him."

The nurse looked to the doctor. The doctor silently nodded and walked from the room.

Mom and Dad made no apologies that their wishes included enlisting God's assistance in the cure and care of their son. Within four hours, Ed's health began improving.

After three weeks, Ed was released from the hospital. The hospital employees were amazed at what they had witnessed and said that there was no logical answer for the turnaround in his condition.

"To us, Faith is a logical answer," Mom casually responded.

Our family's experience with Faith was not made up of biblical story moments. It was more of being a part of something that our ancestors all shared. Being a part of something far bigger than we could ever be on our own.

During Lent, Mom took on the role of the Holy See by granting dispensations for any and all Lenten sacrifices. Each of us would go to her on a regular basis to tell her of our situation and she would (always) absolve you of your commitment for a period of time.

"Mom, as you know I gave up sweets for Lent, however I have been invited to a birthday party…" a question would start.

"The Church recognizes times of celebration and your Lenten obligation is forgiven at that time," she would counsel.

"Mom, on St. Patrick's Day…"

"St. Patrick's Day is recognized by the Church as not having to honor your sacrifices."

"Mom, the school is throwing a banquet on Friday night and they will be serving hamburgers…"

"The Church finds it a much bigger sin to waste food than to eat meat on Friday."

"Mom, I'm going to the Celtics on Sunday…"

"Sundays are a day of rest from your Lenten sacrifice. If you notice they only speak of the 40 days of Lent but if you count the days there are 47, that is because you are not expected to observe your sacrifice on Sundays."

The really amusing part of this was, even though we all knew the answers, we still all go to Mom first to be absolved. I'm talking siblings who are in their 60s would still call Mom to find out if what they were doing was okay. When Mom couldn't be reached, I would call Marsha. Not sure how that worked but the role of the Holy See, in my eyes, fell to the next oldest female in the family.

When I think back to my times in Church, what I remember the most is the laughter. There was a bitter cold day in 1979, when Mom, Dad, Maura and I made our way to St. James the Great Parish in Wellesley. As we stepped into the pew we all started peeling off our heavy coats, gloves and scarves.

At that moment we noticed Mom doubled over laughing at Dad whose coat zipper was stuck. He was caught in a sweltering church with a down jacket zipped to the top so you could only see his eyes protruding over the top. He looked like Mort from the old Bazooka Joe comics.

He would sit patiently as the priest spoke and then, every five or six minutes, he would frantically try and unzip the jacket to no avail. With every attempt brought a new burst of laughter from Mom which made Maura and I laugh uncontrollably. He finally, and frantically, was able to conquer the zipper a mere ten minutes before communion.

Maura and I used to request to sit in different pews for Mass as it made us feel like adults. The problem was, when we got away from Mom and Dad we never acted like adults.

One time in St. Julia's we were messing around and Dad was throwing us daggers from six rows back. We would pretend not to notice and continue on to the point where the person behind us kindly told us we needed to calm down a bit. Being chided by a stranger brought some reality to the situation so we settled in and focused on not making any noise for the rest of Mass.

As timing is everything, as the priest just finished asking for a moment of silence a bee stung me on my neck. I gave a blood curdling scream at the top of my lungs. No one had any idea what was going on. I was seven years old and spun to see my parents who stared at me wide-eyed and in shock as if I had just lost my mind.

The lady who asked us to settle down was raucously laughing thinking I had just decided to go all-in on disrupting the Mass. I'm sure Mom and Dad were experiencing the same thoughts that they had with Mike three decades earlier. "You get him."

"No you better get him."

"If I get him I'll kill him."

"That would still be better for him than if I got him."

"Maybe if we just remain still no one will realize that belongs to us."

When they saw the tears, they knew something was up. Dad got me and brought me next door to the rectory where they wrapped ice in a towel and put it on my neck.

Every Sunday following Mass, when it was not football season, the four of us would go to The Villa in Wayland. The Villa is a quaint little Italian restaurant and one of the waitresses used to wait on Mom and Dad when they went there while dating 40 years prior.

Every Sunday Maura and I would "act up." One Sunday Maura perfectly launched a pad of butter off her spoon into Mom's coffee without either of my parents noticing. It was a thing of beauty that was discussed for years. We watched with joy and anxiousness as Mom sipped her coffee, realizing that something went awry along the way.

Every Sunday we were informed that because of our behavior that this would be the last trip we made as a family to The Villa. The following Sunday, we would be back.

Chapter 27

Mike, Joyce and I sat in the cafeteria. Workers would drift in and out, some looking exhausted, some disgruntled and some sat alone at tables staring blankly at walls just a few feet in front of their face. Added levels of pain could be felt when you heard the bursts of laughter. They unbridled joy that seeped out as they discussed their weekend plans and how they couldn't wait to "get out of here tonight."

Obviously, front line workers cannot, and should not, grieve on your level. It would be impossible for them to wake up and go into work each morning if they were not provided moments of joy to release them from the pain and suffering they are surrounded by each and every moment of their work day.

In the moment, however, it is so hard to step outside of your impending feeling of loss or dread to understand that life does go on and your situation is not even a blip on the radar in their lives.

"So what do you think?" Mike asked.

"I think we are very fortunate to be getting him in a coherent state," I replied. "This is actually a lot more than I was hoping for at this stage."

"What stage do you think we are in?" Joyce asked.

I fumbled with a bag of Nacho Cheese Doritos that I had purchased. Desperately peering inside for a chip that I may have missed. I lightly licked the tip of my right forefinger and jammed it down into the corner to gather as many of the crumbs as possible.

"Pretty late in the game, I think," I said. "It could be minutes, days or even weeks but I think we are witnessing the end of his life."

Mike and Joyce both nodded.

"It's so tough to see him like this," Mike said. "I didn't have to go through this when my Dad died."

We all sat silent for a moment. None of us looking at each other. Each just staring blankly at the counter and wall in front of us.

"That's the thing about heart attacks," Mike continued, "you're not ready for them but you don't have to watch someone deteriorate. I think this is tougher." He paused and turned his head to look towards me and Joyce. "This is much tougher."

Mom, Maura, Jim and Steve came down. They informed us that Dad was being transferred from the hospital to the skilled nursing facility which was next door. We would meet him there in an hour.

"I really think all is going great," Mom said. "Just to think yesterday we were talking hospice and today he is doing so well." I wasn't speaking my mind but felt that we should not discount hospice so quickly.

After finishing our food and talking for a while, we got up to go see how Dad was adjusting to his new environment. Upon entering the room it was as if someone had flipped a switch. He looked great, like a different person. He had some color back in his face. He was sitting up in his wheelchair and eating. He conversed and laughed.

As we stood around his bed, Dad said something about the Kentucky Derby. I was standing at the foot of his bed and said, "That's tomorrow night."

"Huh?" he questioned.

"The Kentucky Derby is tomorrow night," I repeated.

"Oh, that must be a past one they're showing," he said.

I looked over my shoulder at the television that hung on the wall behind me. It was turned off. He either hallucinated a race on that screen or a higher power gave him an insight into tomorrow's race.

As I looked back to Dad he was turned and engaged in a conversation with Mom. I desperately wanted to know who won that race that he saw on the television but the moment was gone. Oh, to only have a bit of divine intervention and the contact information of a local bookie.

Chapter 28

Horse races weren't anything new to Dad. In the 1950s he was a pretty accomplished gambler. At that time he had a very competitive weekly poker game. Seven friends would gather and Dad would almost always be the big winner. He had no fear and would remain calm when faced with a big bet, playing the player's personality far more than calculating the odds of a hand. He could read an opponent and he always played with confidence.

One night they busted him. There was celebration and laughing.

"We got Mac," one of his friends shouted. "We got Mac."

Dad leaned back and took the good natured ribbing. It was deserved. He stood and put his hand in his pocket and felt a crumpled up bill. He pulled it out.

"Hey, you didn't clean me out, I've got a dollar," Dad said.

"I'll cut you for it," his friend said.

They squared up the deck. Dad cut a Jack. His friend cut an eight. "Now I've got two dollars," Dad said. They cut again. He won again. When he hit eight dollars he had enough to get back in the game. He won over $300 that night.

"Don't ever chase a buck." Dad would say over and over through the years. "If you got someone beat, let them leave with dignity. Don't fight them to the death."

Throughout his life he would relax by rifle-shuffling a deck of cards. He always took the time to educate each of his kids on the nuances of the game. At the age of five we would be playing for candy at the kitchen table. He could sense uneasiness. "Scared money always loses," he would instruct. None of us came close to being the level of player he was.

In his gambling heyday, Dad went to Suffolk Downs horse track every day with his system for wagering. The system was simple, he picked the best horse in the race and bet it to show (come in third). This was a viable bet because Massachusetts guaranteed payments of at least ten cents on the dollar. He picked one race and wagered upwards of $200. He was bringing home somewhere between $20 and $40 dollars in winnings every day (which was significant money in the 1950s).

Dad's regular running mate to the track was Freddy Fontaine - a great guy and a free spirit. He was a handyman and a finish carpenter who worked when he needed money. When he saved up some money, he stopped working. "Freddy lived on doughnuts, coffee and cigarettes," Dad said. "And he always weighed 147 pounds."

They met at the Dairy Bell when Freddy was working with a local roofing contractor. Dad needed to find a good handyman because he had no talent at all with tools - a trait inherited by all his children. Freddy would be a part of the McShane family for decades, always on some property or another helping Dad.

The first time they met, Dad was talking about his parents and where they were from. Freddy sipped his coffee and rolled his cigarette between his forefinger and his thumb. "My parents," he said, eyes remaining focused on his beverage, "were in the iron and steel industries."

That took Dad by surprise because Freddy did not give the appearance of coming from money.

"Really," Dad said.

"Yup," Freddy said with a nod. "My mother ironed and my father stole."

They both loved the track and Dad would get a kick out of Freddy on each and every visit. "He would lose $200," Dad said, "and then stop on the way home and not order the meatloaf because it was $1.25. Or if he did order he would always say, 'I would appreciate a generous portion.'"

The daily commute was getting to be too much and Dad approached a local bookie at Patti's Donuts and told him what he was betting and the amounts.

"Yeah Mac, I'll take the action if you don't want to head into Suffolk every day."

After more than a month of Dad's consistent winning, the bookie started to get discouraged by his business arrangement. After one of his payouts the bookie said, "Mac, you're killing me. What are you building, a house?"

Dad picked his horse one day and went over to Duke's Café. The bookie was surrounded by guys getting their wagers in for the afternoon races. Dad glanced at the clock and saw it was noon, his race didn't go off until 3:20 PM. He had plenty of time to get his bet in, he went across the street to his barber, who was also a horse player.

As Dad was getting his hair cut the phone rang. The barber got a tip on the race that Dad was going to bet.

"Mac, you got to switch it up," the barber pleaded with Dad. "This guy is air tight. His information is always right on the money. Every time."

"How many times is every time?" Dad asked.

"Lots," the barber explained. "I don't know how many but I know this guy. He knows what's going on."

"Lots," Dad repeated. "Okay, if he is that reliable I guess information is better than instinct."

The barber's inside information turned out to be very wrong. The horse Dad bet on, the barber's tip, came in last. The horse Dad was going to bet, won. Dad never bet on a horse race again.

"Even though the horse I was going to bet won the race, I knew I had just turned in to a sucker," he explained. "That's how it ends up for everyone. I took a 'hot tip' I relied on 'inside information.'" He laughed and shook his head. "That was the moment I turned. If you are lucky enough to realize when it happens to you, get out immediately."

He respected the games but ended up having contempt for gambling. After the early 1960s he never placed a significant bet again in his life. He was always thankful that he quit gambling before he was making a decent living, "I would have lost everything," he would say casually. "That's why casinos are such big, beautiful buildings. They aren't built because they give money away."

Following my last day of classes at Weston High School, a few buddies and I celebrated by going to Raynham Taunton Greyhound Park. I was betting $2 a race, having a ball, and some of my dogs were doing fairly well.

After the races, I went home and walked in through the garage. I entered the small hallway right by where Dad was sitting with his back to me watching television in his light blue leather recliner.

"How did you do?" he asked without turning around.

"Good," I exclaimed, "I won $18."

"Too bad," he said, remaining focused on the the television.

I assumed he did not hear me correctly because the television was blaring.

"I said, I WON $18," I replied.

He responded, "I heard you, and I said 'too bad' because that $18 is going to end up costing you thousands because now you think you're smarter than the odds-makers."

Yep.

Chapter 29

Following our day with Dad, Maura and I sat at a small table that was positioned on the far end of her kitchen, right next to a window that looked into the patio area of her home. I had a bowl of Honey Nut Cheerios and an orange. Maura had a beer.

We could not stop gushing about how great Dad was in skilled nursing. How it was night and day from when he was in the hospital. This had been an emotionally draining week and we were all just barely hanging on mentally.

"I do have a question, though," I said.

"What?" she asked.

"This whole having a parent who is quite possibly facing an end-of-life situation," I tempered my words because Maura is a great optimist who gets uneasy if she feels someone might be jinxing a situation.

"Yes?" she said with an agonized expression on her face knowing that my conversations can sometimes drift into a ridiculous realm. Especially when I am punch drunk.

"Well," I continued, "Like I said I just got to thinking…and I can't really control what pops into my head…you know?"

"Yes," she responded. Her face now even more contorted with the pain that was about to be released.

I slowly twirled my spoon through the expansive amounts of milk compared to the few Honey Nut Cheerios that still remained afloat. I wondered if it was proper to lift and drink the remaining milk in front of a sibling that you only see once or twice a year? Or should I tirelessly attempt to spoon feed myself small, unsatisfying tablespoonfuls of milk.

"Well, like I said, I just got to thinking that when our parents die, when both of them die, are we orphans?"

"What?" she asked with a bit of exasperation.

"I was just thinking, is the definition of an orphan being someone whose parents have died?"

After my second spoonful of milk, I lifted the bowl to enjoy a satisfying gulp, also blocking Maura's exasperated expression as my eyes became encircled by the bowl.

"No, you have to be a kid to be an orphan," she calmly stated. Her voice resonating from behind my bowl.

"Where does it say that?" I responded while lowering my bowl back down on to the table. "I always thought the definition of being an orphan was that you didn't have parents."

"You have to be a kid," Maura persisted.

"When this occurs, and I hope I'm talking many, many, many years from now, I think I'm going to call myself an orphan," I said.

She shook her head and stared at me like I was a dope.

"I'm going to tell people that you are an orphan too."

"Don't do me any favors," she said as her sentence was sharply cut off by the ringing of her cell phone. She glanced at the number, "Oh no," she softly said as she looked up at me. "It's the nursing home."

That goofing around with the "orphan talk" immediately made me feel like a jerk. You know how people say your life runs past your eyes immediately before you die? Well as soon as Maura said that it was the nursing home I was frozen in place while being flooded with thoughts of my Father.

Was this the call?

Chapter 30

Maura was three years old in 1970, a perfectly normal, healthy and happy toddler. Mom and Dad noticed a slight discoloration in her right eye. Something to be watched but most likely a fever, an allergy or just a change in seasons that caused this occurrence.

The discoloration lingered for a few days but Maura was not showing any other signs of physical ailment or lethargy. Marsha, our oldest sister, noticed some inconsistencies in how Maura would walk and play. She seemed to be favoring her left eye. Marsha went to the kitchen drawer and grabbed a deck of playing cards and asked Maura if she wanted to play a game. Maura cheerily agreed.

Marsha had Maura cover her right eye and flipped a card. She said, "What color is this?"

Maura responded, "Red."

They celebrated the correct answer. Marsha flipped another card.

"What color?"

Maura said, "Red." Correct again.

Marsha flipped another card

"What color?"

"Black." Correct.

Now Marsha asked her to put down the hand covering her right eye and put up her left hand to cover her left eye.

She flipped a card.

"What color?"

Maura peeked out from behind her left hand.

"Black."

"Good," Marsha responded, "but I need you to keep that eye covered Maura." Maura refused. Marsha put her hand up to cover her eye. Maura screeched.

Marsha rushed to Mom and Dad and told them that Maura couldn't see out of her right eye. Mom and Dad raced down the hall to play a much more direct version of the same game. Dad swept Maura up in his arms and covered her "good" eye while Mom held up fingers and they asked Maura how many. Maura squirmed unsure of why she was being put in such impossible situations. They knew Marsha was right. Dad held Maura as Mom frantically dialed the family optometrist, Dr. White. He said to get her to him immediately.

Upon examination, Dr. White, placed a call to Massachusetts General Hospital. He said that Mom and Dad had to get her there now and that he would keep calling to line up the appointments. Maura was admitted instantaneously and had six meetings with doctors that day. The first one said that he thought this was not as serious as first believed. "We're going to run her through a couple of more appointments but I think she's going to be just fine."

Mom and Dad breathed a momentary sigh of relief but each appointment was more involved and each doctor called in others to assist. There was an uneasy feeling that the first doctor was far too optimistic and that this was every bit as serious as they first feared.

By the fourth appointment, a nurse reprimanded Maura, "You will make everything go a lot quicker and easier if you do as you're told."

"She's three and has been in appointments all afternoon. Give her a break," Dad snapped at the nurse. Mom put her hand out and over Dad's arm and eased him back a bit in his seat and she tried to help ease Maura's tensions and encouraged her to participate.

At that moment the first doctor, the optimist, came back in and stoically looked at Mom and Dad and said, "I have bad news. Maura has cancer and a tumor in her brain."

Dad broke down crying. Mom retained complete composure. Life-altering decisions had to be made and she needed to be strong to assure that they were hearing every alternative clearly. The doctor faced Mom and said, "There is no time to waste, within 24 hours the cancer could spread to Maura's other eye and she could be blind. Within 48 hours the cancer could take her life."

Mom and Dad were in a state of shock. They needed a few moments to digest the news and think clearly. They got in the elevator to go downstairs and find a place where they could sit and talk without feeling like the eyes of the world were upon them.

When they entered the elevator a doctor was standing there alone. The only words they had spoken to each other since the doctor spoke was to agree to go downstairs alone to make a decision to treat or not treat. The doctor who briefed them used the word, "could," not the word, "would." However, the doctor was also letting them know that it was an almost definitive, "could." As the doors shut they looked at each other. Dad glanced back at the doctor and back at Mom. She nodded.

Dad turned and reviewed all that just happened to this doctor. They had no idea what he was a doctor of or his level of expertise. They just needed someone who wasn't so emotionally involved to hear what was going on.

As the elevator descended he stood silently and listened. When Mom and Dad were done talking, he paused for a moment and tried to focus them. Clearly, calmly stating, "I would rather have a daughter who is blind in one eye than have a dead daughter." The doors opened at his designated floor. He stepped out of the elevator, reached back to hold the door open with one hand. "Best of luck to you and your daughter." He turned and walked away.

Mom and Dad stood in the elevator staring at one another. Without saying a word, Dad reached over and hit the button to return to the floor they just left. They told the doctor, "Get her into surgery immediately."

Maura lost an eye but kept her life.

A mere few years after that another tragedy was averted when Steve's melanoma was detected by the Marine doctors when he was at Paris Island. There were many moments of Mom and Dad feeling helpless as he lay in a hospital bed in South Carolina.

Mom would, on occasion, excuse herself from the family and head back to her room. My room was next her and Dad's room and on a couple of occasions I went back at nearly the same time. In moments of absolute silence, I could hear the water running in her master bathroom and slight sobs coming from her. No matter our age, Mom would never allow her children to see her cry.

By the time I saw her again, her face would be washed. Makeup would be reapplied and she would be smiling and asking what I wanted to eat. Nothing to see here. Just parents overrun by life.

Mom and Dad stood like mountains during various medical assaults on our family. They led with faith and their belief that no diagnosis was ever the last word. Every medical challenge was a battle the family refused to lose.

Chapter 31

Maura sat transfixed as the phone rang for a third time. She cautiously pushed the button to answer and brought the phone against the right hand side of her face.

"Hello," she said.

"Maura, where are you?" said the voice on the other line.

Maura looked confused, astonished, shocked, full of joy and awe all at once.

"Dad?" she questioned. "Is this you? What's going on?"

"There are bad people here," he said.

Dad did not own a cell phone and he had never called Maura from the skilled nursing facility or the hospital before. In fact, in the history of our family I cannot recall a time when Dad ever made an outbound call. He hated phones the way some people hate liver and onions.

While the warning of 'bad people' was disconcerting, it was also not the first time he had had bouts of paranoia in the last four months. He kept picturing himself in a tough section of Florida, a section where he had never lived. We had researched his prior claims and were satisfied that no one was troubling him; he just had bad images in his head on different occasions. This, we assumed, was one of those times.

Maura handled his call expertly. She soothed at times, was forceful at other times and overall reassured him that all was okay and we were close by.

"The people here don't believe me," he said. "Call the cops."

"I will," she said. Maura looked to me and took a deep breath. It was exhausting trying to appease your father but not wanting to belittle his concerns.

"Don't just yes me," he chided her. "If you don't call the police, you are going to regret this."

"I have to hang up so I can handle this, Dad," she replied.

"Okay," he said. They said their good-byes.

Maura hung up and, while looking down at the table, said, "Great, if anything happens, I'm going to regret it for the rest of my life. Now I've got that to live with."

I knew there were no words that could bring her comfort at this moment so I simply said, "Better you than me."

She tilted her head to face me, gave a pained grin and said, "Thanks."

Chapter 32

Every day of my life, in some form or other, my parents always delivered the message that it was my (our) responsibility to look out for those in need and our family.

It was known in my neighborhood that expectations for our behaviors were held to very high standards at all times and, on occasion, some of the neighborhood kids would get in my face to try to entice me to do things that they know would not be tolerated inside the walls of my home.

In 1977 I was ten years old and the front lawn of my house was the gathering spot for games of fat bat. Fat bat was just what it sounded like, a thick, heavy, plastic bat with which you could crush a Wiffle ball.

We placed home plate out by the street so our split-entry house became the left-field wall at Fenway Park. Line drives bounced off the front of our house afternoon after afternoon. Diving catches and kids sliding into second third and home routinely tore up our front lawn. My parents supported every second of this activity. Yards and homes were to be enjoyed, not used as monuments to how well one was doing in life.

One hot summer afternoon, temperatures on the field began to rise. There were arguments and finger-pointing and kids blaming each other for every mistake imaginable. Basically, it was a typical Saturday.

Except on this day, an older boy in the neighborhood was making Maura the direct target of his attacks. He was twelve and she was seven. And, he was a he and she was a she. The lists that Mom and Dad preached were ticking off in my mind. Don't ever pick a fight with someone younger or smaller than you. Don't ever fight with a girl. Look out for your family. I told him to stop bothering her. He persisted. I told him to stop. He started making fun of me and my sister.

It took me about four running steps to get to him before I launched myself in the air connecting with his upper body and bringing him hard to the ground. He was a couple of years older than me so I needed to get all the advantages I could. Hearing the gasp of air release from his mouth as his head careened off the lawn I knew this was my opportunity to get a few good shots to his head before he could adapt to the situation.

As the gaggle of kids formed around us, each cheering for their favorite participant, we threw awkward rights and lefts. We wrestled and rolled around the ground and slipped in and out of headlocks. We were both slightly bloodied and shaken and, somehow, we separated from one another. To the delight of each and every spectator, we worked our way to our feet and cocked our arms preparing for round two.

At that moment I heard the front door of my house swing open and Dad came bounding across the lawn. "Done," he yelled. "It's over!"

He pointed at the other boy, "Go home, now." Then his head turned and looked at me. "Get in the house," he said softly but with meaning. This was not a time for debate. I turned, head down, and walked to my front door. I could hear the buzz of conversation regarding how I was going to get "it" and how they wouldn't want to be me right now. I agreed, I had no desire to be me at this moment either.

Dad dispatched the neighborhood kids to anywhere other than our yard. "Show's over. Go find someplace else to play." They did as instructed and I could feel him approaching behind me.

As I walked in the house I walked up the staircase and entered the kitchen on the left. It was dark; we did not have air conditioning and there was just a big fan set atop one of the kitchen counters. The shades were drawn to prevent the heat of the sun from pouring in through the bay window.

I slumped down into a kitchen chair knowing that I would cry when I had to answer the first question. Looking back on my childhood, I was a pretty good fighter but I was a crier. Not sure why but the anger emotion was intertwined with the crying valve. My sister came in from outside and she was instructed by Dad to go downstairs to watch TV. Mom stood at the top of the stairs and began to plead my case.

"Gerard, that wasn't his fault," she began but did not have an opportunity to finish.

"I am handling this," he said decisively. "Go downstairs with Maura."

"Gerard," she tried.

"I'm fine," he said. "Just go downstairs with Maura."

Now is probably as good a time as any to say that Dad never once in his life struck me. Through years of disobeying what he said, talking back to both him and Mom and acting like a teenager for most all of my teen years, he never once laid a hand on me. However, he had this magical way of making you feel like today was going to be the day.

He stood in the doorway and listened for the television to go on downstairs. He then motioned for me to sit and said he would be right back. I watched him turn and walk down the hallway.

When he reentered the kitchen he said, "I saw that whole thing."

I didn't look up.

"I saw him picking on Maura," he continued.

Now I looked up, sensing that I might not be in as much trouble as I had feared.

"You stuck up for your sister against an older kid. That's what you're supposed to do," he said as he reached out and stuck a five-dollar bill in my hand. "Don't tell anyone I gave you this, understand?"

I nodded

Chapter 33

Maura and I arrived at the skilled nursing center first thing on Saturday morning. Jim and Steve were picking up Joyce, Mike and Mom and then meeting us at the facility.

We walked in and Dad was sitting in his wheelchair having just finished his breakfast.

"Hi, Dad," Maura said cheerily.

"Hey, Dad," I said right after her.

We stood there with big smiles ready to have a great day.

He glanced up from his food and gave an unwelcoming grin. "I kept asking the question," he began "but no one would answer me."

"What question, Dad?" Maura asked.

Dad looked up at me, "I asked you first, you didn't answer me." He then motioned towards Maura, "She didn't answer me. Joyce didn't answer me. The Other One didn't answer me."

"The Other One" was my brother Steve. It would be a lie if I said anything other than we were finding humor in Dad's inability, at times, to recall Steve's name.

After nearly a full minute of silence Dad said, "Jim looked healthy. He looked good."

Well, of course he did.

Getting deeper into the conversation with Dad we came to realize that the 'bad people' that he thought were in the building last night were men who he thought were going to kidnap Maura and Joyce and sell them into slavery. He was doing all he could to protect them, even from his weakened state and his inability to move from his bed.

His comments to Maura the previous night that she would regret not taking his warnings seriously were those of a father that was in grave fear for his daughters' well-being.

A few minutes later, everyone else arrived and conversation became far less intense. Twenty minutes later one of the rehabilitation folks came in the room to take Dad to occupational therapy. Maura went with him to assist.

Joyce and I wanted to see what kind of workouts he was doing so we gave them a 15 minute head start and then went down to observe his routine. After watching for a while we wandered into an adjoining room and checked out some exercise machines, asked questions of the personnel and made general nuisances of ourselves.

I told Joyce about the previous night's phone call and Dad's fear that she might be abducted and sold into slavery.

She thoughtfully nodded as I told the story. "You know," she said, "at 58 years old, it's kind of a compliment to think that someone might still find me attractive enough to want to sell me into slavery. I honestly don't think there would be too many buyers."

Chapter 34

I was six years old the first time Dad took me to Fenway Park. I don't remember much about that day. Most of my memories of that afternoon probably come more from stories shared over the ensuing years rather than from actual moments in the Park.

Immediately upon entering Fenway we were caught up in a crush of people heading down the ramp toward the concession areas. We turned sharply and made a beeline for the entrance to the field. Dad's hand firmly grasped mine as I avoided the legs of all the people who would not have a clue I was anywhere near them unless they glanced down over their plastic cups filled with beer.

The bright sunlight streamed in to the dark tunnel. I vividly recall the excitement of seeing the baseball diamond of Fenway in person for the first time. We had box seats on the third base side. Dad pointed to the players that I had heard him speak of (or yell at) in front of the television over and over. They were no more than 200 feet from where we stood. Yaz, Fisk, Tiant, Burleson. He would point and say a name. I would ask a lot of questions. He would buy me something to eat to give him a break from the relentless questioning.

He would talk about how Ted Williams played in that outfield, against that left field wall. He told stories about Bobby Doerr and Dom DiMaggio (even teaching me the chant they used to say when Joe DiMaggio came to Fenway:

Who's better than his brother Joe?

No one else but Dom DiMaggio!

I asked him if Dom was really better than Joe. He shook his head no.

He would point to plays on the field and tell me what was happening. I was more captivated by vendors tossing bags of shell peanuts to fans in the stands. Possibly the greatest lesson that he attempted to teach me on that afternoon was how to beat the crowds out of the Park so you did not get stuck in traffic.

Dad was a great crowd escape artist and, by halfway through the seventh inning, he would be headed for the exits. "Always take off while the home team is coming up to bat because all the other fans are waiting until they see them hit."

Invariably we would listen to the ends of games on the car radio as he joyfully escaped from Boston without being snarled in the endless array of cars. I think I was eight years old before I realized you could actually watch the last two innings of a baseball game at the ballpark.

Dad held season tickets to the Boston (then New England) Patriots in section 106. Back when win totals and temperatures both hovered around six. Schaefer Stadium was a windswept bowl which mainly had metal bench seating that you would also find in high school bleachers across the country.

We hated the New York Giants, couldn't stand Don Shula and detested Jack Tatum and the Oakland Raiders. After a while I began to like the Raiders...Dad could not understand this until I explained that they just appeared to be everything that was opposite of the Dallas Cowboys and I really didn't like the Cowboys. That he understood.

The Patriots had a team that teetered on greatness in parts of the 1970s, led by Chuck Fairbanks, Steve Grogan, Sam Cunningham, John Hannah and Stanley Morgan. That team never made the Super Bowl (because of a bogus pass interference call, but that's a story for another book) and many of us wondered if we would ever see our team in the big game. That was long before Bill Belichick decided to resign as the "HC of the NYJ" and use the 199th pick in the draft to select Tom Brady.

As the years went on Dad embraced the comforts of home. He gave up his tickets and brought his passion to the television room for every week of the NFL season. He endured horrible years, celebrated wonderful years and he made it abundantly clear, if you wanted him at a gathering: don't schedule the get-together opposite a Patriots game.

One year, one of the grandkids was being confirmed on a Sunday while the Patriots were playing the Minnesota Vikings. Church was the only thing that would trump football. However, it did not prevent him from saying many times throughout the course of the celebration that followed the ceremony (where the game was on the television), "I'm really surprised that the people in charge of scheduling these things are not aware of when the Patriots are playing. You would think someone over there is a football fan."

The joy of being a fan in Boston was that there always seemed to be a team that was in the mix. The Celtics were dominant in the 60s through the 80s; the Bruins were great in the early 70s and had runs through other decades; the Red Sox had great teams that would routinely break your heart and the Patriots took over the NFL in 2001.

I was in Tennessee on business in 2004 when the Red Sox finally broke through and won their first World Series in 86 years. The moment the game ended, I grabbed the hotel phone and dialed my parents' phone number. Without knowing who was calling, Dad answered the phone saying, "I can now die in peace."

During my formidable years, we would celebrate victories together, mainly the Celtics led by Larry Bird; a bunch of kids from Boston University leading a victory for USA hockey in Lake Placid; and Doug Flutie tossing a Hail Mary against the University of Miami. We would be crushed in heartbreaking fashions, most notably the Sox in '78 against the Yankees and in '86 against the Mets. Then we would revel in Boston's sports dominance that began in 2001. We agreed that the victories were so exhilarating because we suffered through all the pain.

Through it all sports brought us together. It was conversation when we were at ages that we wouldn't know what else to talk about. It was a common ground when we weren't agreeing on anything else. It was a connection during times when I otherwise felt alone.

Chapter 35

Dad finished his workout. The physical therapist was encouraged. "He's really doing well," she said. "You can tell when someone is actively trying to improve and he is."

She looked back towards him in his wheelchair. "I was just saying how well you are doing." He nodded without much of an expression. She told him when he would come back but it didn't resonate. He knew someone would bring him down the hall when it was time to come back.

We were slowly walking back to his room with Joyce pushing his wheelchair.

"Stop" Dad said.

We stopped and Maura said, "What's up?"

"We have to go back and tell her," Dad said.

Maura looked perplexed. "Tell the physical therapist?" she asked.

"Yes," Dad replied.

"Tell her what?" Maura asked.

"That Jim's dead," he said.

"Jim who?" Maura asked.

"Jim McShane," Dad said.

"Jim's not dead, Dad," Joyce said. "We are going to go see him right now. He's down with Ma and everyone else."

"Oh," Dad said. "Okay."

None of us had any idea where that came from or what all of a sudden prompted him to say anything along those lines.

Maura raised her eyebrows and whispered, "Oh, boy."

I turned to Joyce and said, "I get to tell Jim."

"No," Joyce said, "Please, please, please let me tell him."

"I called it," I said coldly and decisively.

Come on, who doesn't like knocking down the favorite child a couple of notches? And what could be better than, "by the way, Dad thinks you're dead."

"Let me have this one," Joyce persisted. "Please, let me have this one."

I relented, "Only because tomorrow is Mother's Day, consider it my gift to you. You tell Jim."

"Yes," she said, almost giddy.

We walked Dad back down to the outside, patio area that had large glass windows overlooking the small pond out back. Everyone was sitting in the room, except Jim.

"Where's Jim?" I asked.

"Out talking to one of his kids," Steve said.

Jim has five children, and each one of them calls him almost on a daily basis. Joyce already was making a break for the door.

"Wait for me," I said, "You can tell him but I get to be there."

I leaned in and told Steve the story before going through the door. As Joyce and I started down the hallway, Steve was knocking on the glass window of the door.

"I should get to tell him, I should get to tell him," Steve said through the window. "I've taken the biggest beating down here."

We shook our heads no and walked quickly down the hallway. As we were about to head outside, the door swung open and in walked Jim.

"Oh, do we have a story for you," Joyce said.

Jim looked to me. I stood smiling and nodded. He smiled, with apprehension. Being a McShane, until you hear a story you are never quite sure if you are going to love hearing about how someone else got tormented or if you are actually the butt of the joke.

Joyce relayed the story in perfect detail and nuance.

"Me?" Jim said, putting his head in his hands. "I'm the one who's dead?"

"Only the good die young," I said.

"Wait a second," Jim said, "Now I'm starting to get a little bit nervous. Yesterday he saw a halo around my head and a door opening up from the ceiling and today I'm dead. This may be a bad omen."

We laughed. "We couldn't wait to tell you," Joyce said.

"Well I'm glad you're both enjoying this," Jim said.

Chapter 36

By 1977 Dad was at a professional crossroad. He had disliked the oil business for all of his adult life. At 52 years old he realized that he either needed complete control of McShane Oil or to outright sell the business to his longtime partner, Richie Sutherland.

While some of us were very attached to the name on the side of the truck, Dad always thought of family before objects. Yes, his father had started the business as an immigrant with no assets to his name and the two of them had built it up over decades. However Dad looked forward, he was concerned that his sons were going to talk themselves into it being their duty to carry on the family business - as he had convinced himself over and over throughout his career. He was determined to do what was best for his family. Either sell the business for the right figure or take complete control and focus on building a bigger brand with a larger footprint.

When he approached his partner, Richie, he found they were on the same page. Richie said, "Gerard, I was going to come to you with the exact same proposal." The time was right for this partnership to end.

The selling of the business went as smoothly as their decades long partnership. Every morning they started their day at Patti's Donuts. Dad would get a cup of regular coffee and a jelly donut. Richie would do the same. They would sit across from each other and discuss their daily responsibilities.

After deciding that it was time to dissolve the partnership, they knew there was only one way to do it. They met at Patti's and sat across from one another at a small table. Neither had any papers in front of them and the normal flow of customers ambled in and out. A few regulars stopped at the table to say hi.

Richie said, "Okay, let's get started."

Dad nodded, "I'll give you $20,000 for your half of the business."

Richie responded, "I'll give you $25,000 for your half."

Dad, "I'll go to $30,000"

Richie, "I'll go to $35,000"

People kept walking around them, greeting them. They sipped their coffee and ate their donuts, each knowing that one of their lives would change forever by the time this cup of coffee was gone.

The bidding dropped to $1,000 increments, and then $500 increments. They each knew the number was close. Richie made a bid.

Dad extended his hand across the table and said, "Congratulations."

Richie smiled and shook his hand, "Thanks."

"The deal is done at that number," Dad said. "But I've got to know."

"How much higher I would have gone?" Richie asked.

Dad nodded.

"$1,000. Then it would have been yours."

They each had, essentially, the exact same valuation on the business. They handled their transaction with respect and as gentlemen.

The following year the Blizzard of '78 hit Massachusetts. Dad was sure that McShane Oil made a lot of money but you could not pry the grin off his face for not having to go out and battle that winter on a daily basis.

He sat downstairs in his recliner, watching the 25" console television situated on an angle in the far corner of the room and would look to his right at the snow drifts piling higher and higher against the sliding glass doors heading out into our backyard. He would softly laugh and say, "I wonder what Richie is doing right now."

Chapter 37

We walked back down the hall with Jim and entered an enclosed patio. It was a large space with windows overlooking beautiful grounds. It was usually occupied by various families grouping in different corners but, today, we had the area to ourselves and moved the chairs in a circle.

It was on this patio on this random Saturday afternoon that something shocking and unforeseen happened. Dad was Dad again. His personality and engagement was fully there and strong. He laughed and conversed. He was dictating and fully immersed in each conversation.

"Where's my Red Sox cap?" he asked.

"It's at home," Mom said. "I keep forgetting to bring it over."

"I want that cap," he said. "That cap gets a lot of attention."

"What kind of attention?" Steve said.

"When I wear that I get a lot of positive comments," Dad said, "Alright Boston! Let's go Red Sox! I like that hat."

"You probably wouldn't get the same type of positive statements with a Patriots cap," I said.

"Yeah, well, who cares? I'd still wear it," Dad said.

We took pictures. Our family never takes pictures but the siblings and extended family members who were in Naples and up in Massachusetts wanted visuals and we were clicking away. Dad asked to see the pictures and marveled at the iPhone technology.

"Everyone looks great," he said. "I look like a ghost."

"You don't look like a ghost," Mom said. In actuality, his description was accurate. His color remained off. Very pale and almost a slight grayish hue.

"Look at me," he said. "I need to get some sun."

Those interactions showed us connection and a thought pattern by him that was saying that he plans to stick around a while longer. Vanity is a positive sign; it shows you are still in the game.

Being Kentucky Derby day, our conversation naturally went to the big race which was going to be taking place in a matter of hours. My brother Steve, who continuously provides self-deprecating jokes about his weight, teed one-up for Dad.

"Dad," Steve said, "Do you think I could become a jockey?" He rubbed his round stomach and smiled.

Dad looked at him and nodded. "Sure," he said, "of a dinosaur."

The room erupted in laughter.

Joyce asked Dad a few questions about gambling at first but then some more specific questions about Dad's family growing up.

A few minutes later he repeated the answers he gave her to me but prefaced it by saying, "Like I was saying to the interviewer…"

Joyce's head rapidly turned back and forth like it was on a swivel.

"Wait a second," Joyce said. "Am I the interviewer? Am I the interviewer?" She leaned forward in her chair, back arched with her arms outstretched and her palms facing upward. "I asked a couple of questions and now I'm the interviewer?"

I was laughing and walked over to where Steve was sitting. Everyone in the room could tell that Dad was sizing him up for another one-liner.

Steve spoke softly to me, "I know I set him up with that jockey line but I wasn't expecting that good of a comeback."

"You're in his sights," I said.

Steve stood, turned to his profile and stuck out his stomach. "The weight's not that bad, right Dad?"

Dad shook his head and said, "You are just barely on the fringe of being human."

As we all laughed, Dad glowed. He was not an object lying in a bed to be pitied. He was not idly biding time waiting for death. He was the center of attention; he was cracking everyone up. He was Dad.

That patio was magical.

Chapter 38

There was Dad, a relatively young man at 52, having sold the business that he had been working at since age 12. All of his dreams and nightmares coming true in one relentless gush of nothingness. No responsibilities. No 2:00 a.m. calls. No trucks breaking down. But also no purpose.

He couldn't just become a human pillow, sitting atop a comfortable chair in the television room for the rest of his life. His desire to become a real estate broker had waned. No need to continue to give up his weekends and holidays. Dad quickly became bored. While retirement sounded great, he needed to be needed.

One of the first things that happened around this time was he acquired a small apartment building in Newton. This wasn't actually a part of the plan. Okay, there was no plan, but if there had been a plan, this wouldn't have been a part of it.

Dad had a very close friend that was a prominent real estate investor and speculator. They had done a couple of deals earlier where they went in on properties together. Years prior, this investor contacted Dad and asked if he could borrow $25,000 as he was underwater on a couple of properties and needed to make some payments to the bank. His word was solid, "Whenever you need the money, Gerard, I'll have it to you within 24 hours."

The deal made sense for Dad. The investor was going to pay him more of a return than Dad would get in the bank but less than what he would have to pay if he borrowed the money directly. Dad lent him the money.

Dad called in the debt after the money floated for nearly a year. Dad said, "The 24 hours wasn't necessary, within 30 days would be fine."

"Sure," the investor said enthusiastically. "Actually, are you available tomorrow? I won't have the money by then but would love to grab lunch and catch up."

Dad agreed.

Dad sat in a corner booth. The investor walked in and across the diner. He got to Dad's booth. Dad looked up and gave a welcoming grin.

"He got to the booth and cleared his throat," Dad said. "If someone comes in clearing their throat, it's going to be followed by bad news."

"I can't get you the money right now, Gerard," the investor began. "The real estate in this area is killing me and all that's going on in the world, but I'll have it to you soon. You have my word."

Dad replied, "I know you're good for it and I said it didn't have to be within 24 hours. Take the 30 days."

The investor took 30 days…then 30 more…then 30 more. There was still no reimbursement of funds. Sightings of the investor became fewer and further between. He stopped frequenting the diners and restaurants where they used to meet and when they did run-in to each other, the investor was always late for an appointment and needing to get back to Dad in "a day or so."

After two years Dad learned that the investor had recently built an apartment building in Newton. Dad found out where he was going to be and confronted him on his new property. Dad said, "I understand that cash is tight. So why don't I take over that property and we'll just put the money you owe me towards the down payment."

The investor nodded and said, "Gerard, I think that's a great solution." He extended his hand and gave a nice, firm handshake with a smile.

At the conclusion of signing all the closing paperwork, the two men shook hands once again and said they would need to grab dinner soon. The investor left the lawyer's office. Mom turned to Dad and said, "You know he's never going to talk to you again, right?"

"What are you talking about?" Dad asked.

"He will never speak with you again," she repeated flatly. "You can tell just by the way that he spoke and smiled. He wants nothing to do with you."

Dad had spent a lifetime reading people. He knew she was way off on this assessment. Dad gave a slight laugh with a shake of his head and said, "You're crazy. We've been friends for decades and all he was doing was getting a loan repaid. If anyone should be upset it's me."

The investor never spoke to Dad again.

Chapter 39

Saturday afternoon was drawing on and Dad began to get worn down. We decided that it would be best if we visited with him in shifts for the rest of the day. So half stayed with him at the hospital and half of us went to Mass down the street.

Upon our return, we found Dad propped up in his bed. Joyce, Mike and Steve took their places on his right side and Jim and I stepped to the left. The pre-Derby race pageantry was taking place. The horses were being paraded as the trumpeter played My Old Kentucky Home.

"I like the gray horse," Dad said.

"Number nine?" Steve asked.

"Yes," Dad said.

"Did you pick that one because it's Ted Williams' number?" I asked.

"No." Dad said. "Whenever I went to a track and didn't know anything about the horses or the jockeys and couldn't get my hands on a program, I'd always put a little money on the gray one."

We talked as the race went off. No one had a betting interest so we all rooted for horses we randomly selected and shared the moment with Dad.

None of our random picks came in the money…much the same result as if we had a betting interest.

After the Derby we scanned the television stations, trying not to tax Dad with too much conversation. I stopped on the Barrett Jackson Car Auction.

"That's a '41 Ford," he said before the make or model was flashed on the screen and he was correct. "That's a '56 Chevy," he stated and was again correct. Car after car came up on the screen and he was calling them all out.

He was getting tired. His eyes fluttered a few times and finally they closed but he wasn't asleep. He was still engaged.

"What do you think the nicest looking car Mike ever owned was?" I asked him. My brother Mike had some beautiful cars back in the early to mid 1960s.

"The '57 T-Bird was really nice but I think the best looking was the '63 Corvette," Dad said, his eyes firmly closed.

Joyce sat to my left watching the conversation. Her husband, Mike stood by the right side of the bed. Steve and Jim were now by the foot of the bed.

"You could get a car for pretty short money back then, couldn't you?" I said.

"Yes," Dad replied.

The television camera lost its signal momentarily and Dad's eyes opened with the jolting sound of static.

"My Father would sit and watch that for hours at a time," he said with a small laugh shutting his eyes again.

"Watch what?" Joyce asked.

"The static," he said. "He bought the first television on the street. There were only two channels."

"What year was that?" Joyce asked.

"1951," he said.

"How much did the television cost?" Jim asked.

"$1,200."

Joyce came out of her seat. "$1,200 in 1951?"

Dad nodded. In this light an indent on the left-hand side of his head that was caused by his loss of weight was prominently displayed.

"How much would a new car have cost then?" I asked.

He thought for 30 seconds, his eyes opened so he could stare at the ceiling. "A new Chevy or Ford would have probably gone for about $675."

"So he could have had two new cars for the price of a television," I said.

He grinned and nodded. His breaths were becoming more elongated. Our conversation tapered off and he drifted to sleep. We felt guilty getting up to go while he slept. We wondered what his reaction would be when he awoke and we were not there but we also realized that he might very well be out for the night.

As we walked out, Steve, Jim, Joyce and I stood a foot into the hallway, looking back into the room through the door at Dad lying there. Out of the corner of my eye, I noticed Mike standing, his back against the wall looking towards us and then down at the floor. In silence, we turned and walked down the hall together.

Chapter 40

The toughest part of -an early retirement for Dad was that he desperately missed people. He always liked to portray himself as not wanting to go to parties or weddings (or anything that required a tie) but at his core, he loved conversation and was always informed about the day's events.

He found what he thought was the ideal solution. He was going to buy a sub shop with his nephew, Bobby Millar. Dad knew his culinary limitations - they pretty much began and ended with pouring a bowl of cereal. He also knew that Bobby and his wife Emily had the food preparation talent. Dad had the initial investment.

The place they purchased was called Corratos. The previous business was the same as what they were opening. A sub shop that also did some catering. Always tough to open the exact same business on the site of a failed business with the only change being, "our stuff tastes better than their stuff" business plan. They knew they needed another change. Embracing a strategic marketing epiphany that will never be taught at the top business schools, their grand idea was to rename the establishment "Lorratos" (they only had to pay the sign painter to change the first letter).

The business was located in Newton, Massachusetts, and the quality and portion size quickly made this little business a go-to location for the local neighborhood and business people. Bobby and Emily worked tirelessly in the back of the house preparing all the food and Dad greeted customers, took orders and worked the register. Lines would extend out of the small shop and down the street at lunch time. It was fun, busy and an enjoyable work environment.

Unfortunately the size of the establishment limited the amount of revenue that could be generated. Dad knew that Bobby and Emily were the drivers of Lorattos' success and they had a young family they needed to support. He sold his ownership stake to them and was, once again, on the hunt for a new "retirement" job.

He was getting hounded by financial experts on the need to greatly increase his net worth and to have income generation vehicles that would create the same income as if he was still working. He thought most of them were nothing more than bookies working the races. "They've got a no lose situation," he would say, "you buy a stock, they get paid, the market goes up or down and you sell the stock, they get paid. Nothing more than the vig the house collects on every wager when you're gambling."

He would be very frustrated watching friends get taken by some of these investment advisors. "They all tell me how much the stock went up. They don't factor in what they're paying in commissions," he would lament. "A lot of them don't even know what they're paying in commissions!"

At his core, he was an everyday person who was happy with everyday things. He thought financial advisors scared people out of ever being able to retire or enjoy their lives. "Most financial advisors are dead wrong," he would say. "They tell you there is no way you can comfortably live the rest of your life without vast sums of money. That's because most of them have vast sums of money and think that everyone wants to lead an elegant lifestyle. You want to get by just fine in life? Don't buy something if you don't have the money in the bank."

Another great frustration Dad found in retirement was now he needed a credit card. He hated everything about credit cards. He paid in cash and never owed anybody anything. However, with their freedom from the oil business Mom and Dad were spending a good deal of time down in Florida and hotels were only accepting credit cards for the down payment.

At the age of 53, Dad relented and applied for a card. He was promptly rejected. He had no income because he had sold his business the previous year and that's all the information the companies were looking for at that time. He applied to another credit card company. The rejection came so fast he mused it might have passed his application in the mail.

Two more applications and two more rejections. He was exasperated. Here was a couple who had done everything right their entire lives and always lived well below their means and, having lived such a conservative manner, they didn't have a credit history of which to speak.

He and Mom made copies of their savings and real estate holdings and sent them to a credit card company. Within a week they were contacted with the "great news" that they had been approved for a gold card, which would give him a credit limit of $10,000…blah, blah, blah. He was even more exasperated.

He called the company to try and explain, "I don't want a gold card," he calmly said.

"But sir, do you realize that the gold card…" the salesman tried to explain.

Dad broke in, "I don't even want a credit card. I just want to rent a hotel room. That's it."

Throughout their lives, that's really the only times that credit card left his wallet. He thought credit was a very dangerous thing that most people couldn't manage or handle.

Transitioning from the sub shop turned out to bring Dad the most professional joy that he ever had. He accepted a position at Bentley College as Equipment Manager, working Monday through Friday from 1:00 p.m. until 9:30 p.m., managing the gym and pool.

Dad was surrounded by young, vibrant, people. He loved watching the games in the gym, talking sports with the coaches and students. He did what he did best; he helped guide young people with common sense to try and get them to understand the importance of enjoying their life and not becoming overwhelmed by school or life.

He was a magnet for students and professors alike. You could not go into his office without someone being in there looking for help. And there he would sit in his blue, Bentley Athletic polo shirt, yellow shorts, white sneakers and socks. Always smiling. Always ready to help.

It was the perfect "retirement" job.

Chapter 41

Sunday morning, Mother's Day, found Dad sitting up in his bed, pushing this morning's breakfast around his plate without much interest.

"How's breakfast?" Maura asked him.

He shook his head. "Not good."

"Do you want us to get you something else?" Mom asked.

"No," he said, his eyes glanced around the room a bit at us and then focused in on Mom. "I'm fine."

"Are you sure you ate enough?" Mom persisted.

His eyebrows rose a bit and his head bobbed in a small nod, "I'm fine." He was letting everyone in that room know that he was still more than capable of knowing whether or not he had an acceptable amount of food. It can be easy to forget that diminished health does not necessarily equate to an inability to inform how their life is best lived.

Mom, Maura and I stood by his bed while Steve and Jim went into the hallway to allow a nurse's aide to get Dad cleaned up and remove his tray.

The young man picked-up my Dad's tray and turned to leave.

"Thank you," Dad said.

"You are welcome, sir," the aide responded.

As the aide turned from the room and began walking down the hallway, Dad said softly in a mockingly formal voice, "Thank you for bringing me this crap."

Maura and I busted out laughing.

Mom said, "Gerard, watch what you're saying, other people are in this room." She tilted her head to point to a nurse who was helping the gentleman in the next bed.

He just stared for a moment at the people Mom referenced. Neither turned as they were engaged in getting his roommate ready for the day. He then glanced back at me and Maura and watched us continue to laugh.

Sensing he could use a change of scenery, and needing more space for all of us to gather, we brought Dad out to the lounge area of the building. This space near the front reception was very welcoming with high, vaulted ceilings, light pastel colors on the walls and comfortable, cushioned seats. It had a warm, southern, feel.

Being Mother's Day, the focus shifted from Dad to Mom. This was the first time in 25 years that any of us, other than Maura, were with her on Mother's Day. Everyone else had mailed a card to her, but since I am horrible with cards I was handing her the one I had picked out. If I remember to buy a card it usually sits on a kitchen counter until the big day arrives and then I'm throwing it in the mail that afternoon.

This was one of those occasions when I bought the card two weeks in advance, filled it out, sealed and dropped it on the counter and let it sit. When everything came to a head, I grabbed the card, threw it in my luggage and left.

The note I had written Mom was now mistimed and totally inappropriate. It was saying how I hoped Dad was enjoying his new living environment and how I heard everything was going great for Mom. She laughed as she read the message and handed the card to Maura to show what I had written. What a difference a couple of weeks makes.

Our conversation turned to the greatest television shows of all time. There was some ranking of the 100 best series that were ever aired and it became a hotly contested debate in our circle.

Dad sat in his wheelchair, methodically looking down and buttoning up his gray sweater. His hands worked their way down the front searching for buttons that were still loose as he listened to the debate.

"The two best shows of all time," he interjected, "are All in the Family and Seinfeld."

"I put Twilight Zone and Breaking Bad up there too," I said.

"Twilight Zone was great," he agreed. "I never saw Breaking Bad."

He looked back down and continued to button his sweater.

"What did the report say was the best show of all time?" he asked.

"Friends," I responded.

He looked up, squinted a bit and shook his head, "That's a terrible call. Friends? That wouldn't even make my top 100."

Mike had stepped outside, came back and said that it was beautiful. We asked Dad if he would like to go out and get some air. He nodded, "Sounds good."

We all stood. Dad fumbled with a button on his sweater. He didn't want help but he did want it buttoned and it was not cooperating.

Chapter 42

I was seventeen years old in 1984, a Junior at Weston High School and failing miserably at finding my identity. Inside of me was this extrovert who liked to speak and crack jokes and wanted to be loud, but I was completely bogged down with self-doubt and a feeling like I just couldn't fit in.

My search for an identity brought me through a Bruce Springsteen phase, jeans and not shaving for a few days; an athletic phase; a leather jacket phase (not really sure if that was a Hell's Angels or a Fonzie phase - neither resonated). Dad could see these shifts and at times he would just tell me to be myself. "As people get older they see who the decent people are. You'll be fine, just give it time."

Other times Dad's instructions were far more direct.

I woke up late one Saturday morning, walked down the hall and into the kitchen. Dad sat at the end of the kitchen table reading the Boston Globe.

"Morning," I muttered.

"Good morning," he said as he glanced up from his paper.

I'm not sure what photograph or article caught his attention that particular morning but he followed his morning salutation by saying, "You know, I see a lot of boys at Bentley that get that earring in one ear and I know it's a thing now."

"Uh, yeah," I said sort of still asleep and extremely confused.

"I just want to let you know that if you ever decide to do that, I'm not going to say a word," he said as his eyes drifted back down on to The Globe.

I stood in the doorway dumbfounded. I had no desire to get an earring but to hear this man that I thought I knew so well express his openness to the fashion and culture of today was truly something that I never thought I would experience. Maybe he really did understand how tough it is to fit in. Maybe he really would support me in whatever I needed to do. "Really?" was all I could muster.

Without raising his eyes from the newspaper he said, "Really. I'll walk across the room and rip it out of your head, but I won't say a word."

Ahhhhh, there he is. There's Dad.

I laughed and continued on past him to the refrigerator. If I had ever done it, he would not have touched the earring or me. However, he had a forceful, humorous and memorable way of getting his points across.

One of the great misconceptions in life is that growing up with strict parents is difficult. I always felt the exact opposite; "cool parents" shift all the burden of responsibility on to their kids. When your parents are strict, the blame always begins and ends with their decision-making.

Cool parents force kids to grow up fast. Strict parents allow the opportunity to hang on to childhood for as long as possible. Sure there are rules, boundaries and guidelines but all you have to do is follow them.

In my house the strictness was clearly defined. Grow your hair long; I'm not going to be happy. Don't shave for a few days; we're going to talk. Think about getting an earring or (God forbid) a tattoo and they will guarantee that there is another very different thought coming by shortly to jar that one loose.

After my high school graduation I grew a full beard and mustache. One Saturday night I went to church with Mom and Dad. As we walked in, Dad turned to me and said, "Why don't you sit in a different pew."

"What?" I asked in disbelief.

"You look like a bum," he said.

I glanced up at the picture of Jesus on the wall behind me in full beard and mustache and just pointed.

"It was a different time," he said.

I sat in the same pew.

There was a code of conduct. You did not wear a hat indoors, you held doors, you showed respect, you help those who are less fortunate and you always looked out for your family. And if looking out for your family put you in an uncomfortable situation then that's the situation you were destined to be in at this point in your life. "Don't ever start a fight, you're better than that," Dad would say, "but don't walk away from a fight if you know you're fighting for what is right."

Strict parents have conversations; it's not a dictatorship but the boundaries were generally based around the law or a moral code so there wasn't a lot of room for argument. We were given a lot of trust and were regularly asked if we thought something was a good idea or if we should be hanging around with certain people. If we gave the wrong answer we were redirected to the right answer. If we broke a trust, it took a while to rebuild.

They were strict but they always had our back IF we deserved it. If we did something mean or disrespectful towards someone, we were never let off the hook without making things right. We were held accountable to a higher standard than others. Mom and Dad always said if they ever caught us doing anything illegal, they would be the first one to call the police.

In time, we realized the compliment that it was that they expected so much more from us than they would expect from others.

Chapter 43

We took over half of the front porch. It was perfect, 71 degrees, sunny with a beautiful light breeze.

Steve played the role of the straight man once again. He would serve up softball opening lines to Dad and let him knock them out of the park. We had found health, spirit and a sense of control in humor.

Joyce turned to Steve and whispered, "I think you've added six months to his life."

There was no disagreeing with that sentiment. Humor was providing Dad a purpose, it was challenging him to quickly use his brain and be a participant.

"How many times have you seen Gunga Din? I asked him.

"Over 70," he said. "And I'll probably see it 70 more times."

There is no movie that resonated with Dad more than Gunga Din. It's the story of a water boy in India who serves the soldiers as they go off and fight. He is nothing more than an after-thought of the soldiers, just a carrier of their nourishment. However, in the end, he sacrifices everything for them, looking not for glory but simply doing what he sees as what is right and necessary.

Dad could recite the full 85 line poem by Rudyard Kipling verbatim, however, it was most common to hear him utter the final two lines:

By the livin' Gawd that made you,
You're a better man than I am, Gunga Din!

"The other movie that was amazing when it came out was King Kong," Dad said. "The special effects were absolutely incredible."

"What year did King Kong come out?" Joyce asked.

"1933," he responded. I visualized my Dad at eight years old running down the streets of Waltham with his buddies to see the amazing King Kong.

I thumbed through pictures on my iPhone to show Dad a recent shot of Theresa and our kids on top of the Empire State Building.

"We just went to New York city last summer," I said.

He looked at the picture, "Amazing," he said, "that's great."

Steve leaned in and said, "I was thinking about going to New York City to the top of Empire State Building but didn't know if it was such a good idea."

Dad immediately responded, "If you tried that everyone would probably start yelling, he's back. Kong is back."

Dad wasn't missing the easy one-liners. The change in the last couple of days was amazing. While he was obviously weakened and impaired he was far more the man we always knew, it was this incredible glimpse of the man he always was before the illness had wreaked havoc on his body. 48 hours ago we didn't think this was a possibility.

"Remember the old Bob Newhart funny phone calls?" I asked him. Bob Newhart in the 1960s had a comedy album comprised of fictional phone calls where you only hear Newhart's half of the call. In each he put himself in a famous situation.

He started to laugh, "Those were great," he said. "The security guard of the Empire State Building that was on his first night of duty as Kong was climbing the building."

Dad lifted his hand to the right side of his head and began doing a part of the routine. "Yes sir. I did check the manual sir but this doesn't seem to be covered anywhere in there."

"How about the Sir Walter Raleigh routine?" I said.

He kept his hand at the right hand side of his face and flowed into the routine, "So you take the leaves, shred them up and roll them into a piece of paper…don't tell me Walt, don't tell me, you stick it in your ear, right?"

We then talked about the person who impersonated John Fitzgerald Kennedy in the early 1960s but none of us could come up with his name. Dad was thinking.

"I'll look it up online," Steve said, pulling out his phone.

"No," Dad said his eyes closed, "give me a minute."

He opened his eyes, "Vaughn Meader," he said with authority. "Poor guy, he was very popular and then when Kennedy was assassinated, his career just ended immediately."

Dad was right. He was absolutely battling short-term forgetfulness and confusion but his long term memory was going on all cylinders.

Chapter 44

In 1984, the start of my senior year in high school, one of the management professors came in and sat down in Dad's office. Dad went to war and never got around to college. However he was always sought out by successful business people because of his calm demeanor and common sense approach to any deal.

He was a ferocious negotiator and had the bluffing ability of a seasoned poker player but he was eminently fair. He always searched for the best possible outcome for both parties. His attitude was that if everyone won, you would be more likely to help each other again in the future.

"So, Jerry," the professor questioned (Dad spent his entire life being called Gerard but the folks at Bentley started calling him Jerry and that's what people called him ever since), "where's Patrick looking to go to school?"

Dad was filing papers in his desk drawer and was a bit more preoccupied with where he left the folder he needed than with answering the question. After a few moments he glanced up and focused. He said, "He wants business so he's looking at business schools. Here, Babson, Bryant."

The professor said, "If accepted, I would assume he would go here, correct?"

"They're all good schools," Dad replied. "Wherever fits him best."

"Oh, they're all great schools," the professor quickly agreed. "I just meant seeing as he gets the free tuition here."

Dad's attention was now completely diverted from trying to find that missing folder. "He gets what?"

"Free tuition. He gets free tuition here," the professor repeated. "Are you aware that because you are a full-time employee, Patrick would be eligible to attend Bentley for free?"

"No, I was not," Dad said shaking his head.

"Not a bad little perk," the professor said. "Congratulations, you just hit the lottery."

Dad could have sprouted wings and flown home that night. He came in the house where I was lying on the TV room floor watching a Red Sox game. I looked over my shoulder and up in his direction as he came in the door that connected to the garage.

"Hey Dad," I said.

"Guess where you're going to college?" he gleefully stated.

Chapter 45

The hours were drawing on and we were all well-aware that Mike and Joyce had to leave soon to catch their flight home. We gave some space but there was only so far you could go. I watched from halfway down the walkway and saw Mike lean in and shake Dad's hand.

"So long Jerry, we'll see you in a couple of months," he said.

Dad looked up at him smiling and said, "Okay, have a safe flight."

Mike's hand released Dad's and he stepped one foot behind the wheelchair before he broke down. He quickly walked past me; I reached out my left hand and patted his left shoulder as he continued down the walkway to the parking lot.

Joyce was now saying good-bye. I could not make out the words but saw her lean in and hug Dad. It was a long, lingering hug, near the end I heard her say, "Bye, Dad." They separated, and looked at each other for a moment. She forced a grin on to her face and turned and walked away before crying.

As everyone else was saying goodbye to Mike and Joyce I walked over to Dad and moved his wheelchair a few feet into a spot that was removed from the direct sunlight. He was quiet and stared at the ground, away from me. We made some small talk but I have no recollection what it was about.

My sister and brother-in-law had said good-bye to Dad for the last time, I knew I would be having this same moment in less than 24 hours.

Mom came over and sat down in the chair directly to the right of the wheelchair. She could tell that he was disturbed. I got up and walked to the far end of the porch.

"Are you alright?" Mom asked.

Dad nodded.

"What's the matter?" she persisted.

Dad looked up at Mom. "I could tell Joyce was sad to be leaving me," he said. "I just wanted her to know that I was sad too."

"She knows," Mom said with a quick, confident nod. "She knows."

Chapter 46

If you wandered into the McShane household you generally heard one of four conversations taking place: (1) politics, (2) sports, (3) something regarding the stock market or (4) an interesting obituary. Catholicism was central to our lives but not often discussed. Essentially, if the Holy See said it was so, it was so. No room for debate.

Politics is where battle lines were drawn. Mom and Dad were old-school, Irish, Catholic Democrats who talked about the greatness of Mayor Curley, the remarkable Father Drinan (a Catholic Priest and United States Representative from Massachusetts) and worshiped everything Kennedy. They saw the political parties as good versus evil. Virtue versus corruption. Hope versus greed.

Their politics crept into all areas of their life, almost depriving them of their ability to enjoy something that might benefit people who opposed their viewpoints. For example, their all-time favorite restaurant was Craytons in Florida. They would happily say that, "for $15.95 you would get salad, a main course and dessert." They would remind you that this was, "in the 1970s so this was not inexpensive but the food was fabulous." Yachts would pull up and dock so their passengers could dine.

Craytons would not take reservations and there were always long lines. But it was worth it, Mom and Dad would tell all who cared. They would describe, "Millions of dollars of antiques that lined the walls," and "palm trees that grew inside the restaurant." When they were in Florida they would dine at Craytons at least once a day. You read that right, at least once a day. It was almost perfect. The problem was, right in the middle of this entire splendor, Craytons had a framed picture of Richard Milhouse Nixon.

"The food was so spectacular," Mom said, "we forced ourselves to overlook the picture."

"I never got over it," Dad said.

Every ounce of their being was politically charged. The beauty of their beliefs is that there was no gray area. If you did not share their beliefs, then you did not care about the little guy, the person who needed a hand, the poor or the outcast. They were as protective and supportive of their politicians as they were of their own family members. More so in many areas, because I guarantee you that they explained away behaviors of the Kennedys for which they would have crucified their children.

They would recount in vivid detail being home on Ledgewood Road in Weston when the news broke that President Kennedy had been shot in Dallas. When telling the story they would each freeze in place as they had done on November 22 of 1963. Like the rest of the country, they were immobilized, in complete shock.

More than 50 years later the weight of their despair was still apparent as they described sinking into chairs, eyes transfixed on the black and white images flickering across the television screen. They hung on every word, waiting to hear more about the updates on their president and his would-be assassin.

They prayed for the President's well-being. The kids came home from school asking if my parents had heard what had happened to the President. They still spoke with disdain about Marsha telling them that two kids on the bus were laughing and said that their families never liked Kennedy anyway. The family sat together and watched Walter Kronkite confirm the worst news they could have imagined, that John Fitzgerald Kennedy was dead.

Mom and Dad doubled down on their beliefs and strongly supported Robert Kennedy for president and Ted Kennedy for Senator. Mom volunteered on Robert Kennedy's team and was equally devastated when he, too, was assassinated.

I remember working on crafts projects at the table with Mom while the Nixon tapes were playing out of our large, console radio and record player. We screamed at the television together during the 1980 Democratic Convention to allow Ted Kennedy an opportunity to run in the primary against Jimmy Carter. We were proud and loud Democrats.

Politics became a far more interesting and combative conversation as my political leanings became more conservative. My roots in the Catholic Church, amongst other beliefs in economic and military policies, led me to the Republican Party. My parents could not understand, or appreciate, my political independence from their point of view.

Political arguments started getting especially heated in 1985, my freshman year in college. Dad battled me on issues and backed his arguments with history ("we are Irish Catholics, Irish Catholics are Democrats"). Mom threw everything against the wall to try to intimidate me into not leaving their allegiances. One of my favorites was her claim that I could never speak in public about my new found conservatism because it would adversely affect the career of my brother who was chief of police in the town in which we lived. She said there was conversation that he might be considered for a bigger state position. She actually kept me off balance for a while.

At the age of 19, I went to the Weston Town Hall and changed my party affiliation from Democrat to Republican. It was the correct decision for me. My parents, on the other hand, were devastated with my new-found affiliation. I was told that I had been brainwashed in other households and that if I was to really care about the unfortunate I would need to come back to the Democratic Party. We argued. We talked. We argued some more.

In November of 1988, I was 21 and finally able to vote in my first election for the President of the United States. This was the moment Mom and Dad had been grooming me for since I was old enough to walk. Unfortunately, the political passions that they instilled within me were backfiring on them. I viewed improving the world differently.

Come election morning in 1988, I was at my parents' house and we were all going to vote. My parents were voting for Governor Dukakis while my support was going to Vice President Bush. We walked in silence to my Father's silver Chevrolet Caprice Classic parked in the driveway. Dad went to the driver's side, Mom to the passenger side and I put my hand on the handle of the back seat car door directly behind Mom.

Dad looked over the top of the vehicle and asked, "What are you doing?"

"What do you mean what am I doing?" I replied with some confusion.

"What do you think you are doing?" Dad repeated as he looked over the top of his car at me.

"Same thing as you," I responded. "I'm going to vote."

"Not in this car you're not," he said calmly. "I'm not transporting any votes for Bush."

"Seriously?" I said.

Well I guess they were because my parents got in the car and started the engine. I stepped to the side and they began to back out of the driveway. I stood, a little bit of me expected them to stop and tell me to get in the car but most of me was enjoying every moment of this exchange and loving the passion around an election.

I walked over, hopped in my Chevy Chevette, and proceeded to follow my parents the entire way to the polls. I parked about 15 spots away from them but increased the pace of my walk so I would be standing right behind them in line at our precinct.

It was with great satisfaction that I took my form knowing that I was heading in that afternoon to nullify Dad's vote.

Over time, Dad and I just didn't discuss politics very much; we both respected but did not fully understand why we each voted the way we did with the beliefs we both shared. I took comfort in the fact that Mom once said to me that Dad told her in confidence that he did not understand my politics but respected the fact that I never hid from my beliefs or backed down to his pressures.

For her part, Mom would regularly call me and say, "I'm sick of agreeing with your father on everything, let's talk politics."

Chapter 47

There was silence for a while. Dad's inevitable demise was brought back to the forefront with the pain of Mike and Joyce's good bye. Mom gave a twitch of her head, motioning for me to come back.

Knowing their conversation was over; I slowly walked back towards their chairs. Not really sure where to go with the dialogue or how to lighten the mood, for them and for me. I decided my best attempt would to be to get him talking about the old days again.

"You were offered a scholarship to Holy Cross, weren't you Dad?" I asked.

He turned to my direction. "Coach Minihan said he couldn't get me one to Boston College but he could get me a full scholarship to Holy Cross to play football."

This was an interesting point about his current condition; he usually wasn't a talker about his accomplishments. He would deflect and shrug and say that a lot of people could have received the same thing. At this point he talked more, and provided some details and didn't always try to minimize his contributions.

"What position did you play?" I asked.

"I was a halfback and a bare-footed punter," he explained. "People used to want to see the kid who would run off the field to quickly take off his shoe and sock to punt a football. I just got a better feel for the ball against my bare foot, it traveled further."

"Were there a lot of bare-footed punters?" I asked.

"Not a lot but I wasn't the only one," he said.

"Why didn't you take the scholarship?" I asked.

"It would have meant a deferral from going into World War II so I declined," Dad explained. It was one of Dad's gifts; he truly saw the world in black and white. There was right and wrong. It was the responsibility of an individual to make the right decision even, especially, if it meant self-sacrifice.

"Do you ever wonder how everything would have turned out if you had taken that scholarship?" I asked.

"No," he said. "Not really. Everything turned out fine. No complaints." Again, there was always the belief that if you made the right choices and worked hard things would find a way of working out.

There was a pause. A cool breeze had drifted in across the front porch of the building and we all drank in the moment like it was a tall glass of lemonade.

"I wanted to serve. Everyone wanted to serve," Dad said. "There was nothing heroic; it was just serving our country."

"How come people aren't like that today?" I wondered out loud.

"They are," he quickly and resolutely responded. "People today would react the same way if the situation was similar."

I silently disagreed. His generation seemed so much greater than mine. They seemed to feel like they were in debt to their country and there was an underlying need to give back.

As my thoughts drifted, Dad continued, "Paris Island was tough but I'll tell you, I put on 14 pounds there. It was the first time in my life that I was having three square meals a day."

"The ones I always felt bad for," he said shaking his head in empathy, "were the ones who couldn't go because of a disability. People looked at them like they were trying to get out of supporting their country but they weren't. They wanted to serve as much as anyone else."

"Some people thought those that couldn't serve were back home trying to steal the girls while so many of the boys were overseas fighting," Mom interjected. "But there really wasn't any of that, probably because we were all committed to the guys fighting the war. The boys that couldn't serve were doing their part however they could with volunteer work and fundraising. Everyone was in it together."

"When we returned home," Dad said, "the whole country treated the veterans with respect. If you went on a bus, people would stand and offer you their seat. A veteran couldn't buy a drink; there was always someone there to pick up the tab."

"Even that didn't encourage you to drink?" I asked. Dad had never touched a drop of alcohol in his life.

"They'd pick up the tab for a Pepsi too," he responded.

Maura walked back from the parking lot after saying her good-byes to Mike and Joyce. Steve and Jim were driving them back to the airport. Maura stood behind Dad and I got up and offered her my chair. She sat and I stood against the wall, looking down towards Dad. He continued to tell stories from his life, including the first time he saw Don Rickles. He said he laughed so hard he fell out of bed.

My left leg cramped up and I wanted to sit down and stretch it out a bit. I walked around the back of his wheelchair and sat on his right hand side, my back against a post and looking up at him. I stretched my left leg directly out in front of me and began to bend until I felt a slight strain on my quadriceps. While doing this I glanced up and realized for the first time this visit, I didn't tower over him. I wasn't looking down upon him or assisting him in some way. My neck was craning upward and he was dictating the conversation.

He continually glanced around but would often look down at me as he spoke. I continued staring, mesmerized.

Everything finally felt right, he was in the position of power and I would follow his lead.

Chapter 48

Alcohol was forbidden in our home for most of my early years. Dad was a teetotaler and Mom might have one or two glasses of wine each year. For decades even the discussion of allowing drinks in for a party would not be considered or tolerated.

Dad's take was that no one knew if they were an alcoholic or not and it might only take one to put you on a very bad course. He would say, "It's nothing except Russian roulette with beer instead of bullets. You can only lose so it's stupid to try."

While they didn't keep any of us completely away from alcohol, some of us (me in particular) were scared off of booze for a long time. I had a legitimate fear of the damages that alcohol could do to me as explained by Dad and an even greater fear of the damage Dad could do to me as explained by Dad.

When my oldest siblings were in their thirties, alcohol was first allowed onto the premises for parties but not yet into the actual home. Through tireless debate, Mom was able to gain a reluctant agreement from Dad to allow a cooler with beer to be placed in the garage. If someone wanted a drink, they could consume the drink in the garage. The following year, alcohol was allowed in the house but only for parties.

Thanksgiving night, 1985, at the age of 18 I decided to grab a late night snack before heading to bed. I rummaged through the refrigerator and pulled out the platter with the remnants of the Thanksgiving meal along with a couple of the sides and the chocolate cream pie. I noticed assorted beers tucked haphazardly throughout the refrigerator as I shifted the plates of food. Undoubtedly, Dad would dump and throw away every last one of these before I awoke the next morning.

A number of beers sprinkled about the lower-shelf were Coors. Whether you drank or not in the northeast at that time, Coors caught your attention because it was considered to be bootlegged east of the Mississippi. Years earlier every boy who saw Smokey and the Bandit envisioned themselves hauling around in a sweet Trans Am with a wild Sally Field by their side and blocking for Jerry Reed who was running a truckload of Coors across the state line.

I glanced and saw bags of empty beer and soda cans untied on the back staircase. I thought that if I ever did decide to drink, it would be pretty cool to say my first beer was a Coors. It might be my only shot to ever have one, I reasoned. I snuck it back to my room and drank it down while eating my third Thanksgiving dinner of the night. It was gross and I longingly wished for a Coke to wash this nastiness down. I snuck the bottle in with the other empties and no one was the wiser.

The following summer I had a few Bartles & James wine coolers while shooting baskets at a friend's house. That was it for my drinking, until the summer following my 20th birthday. The floodgates opened up that summer and my experimentation with alcohol grew. Somehow the beer manufacturers must have improved their formulas because it was no longer gross. It was the sweet nectar of the Miller Brewing Company gods.

One night a friend picked me up to go to a party in Framingham, a town located about fifteen minutes west from where I lived. The party flowed from inside to outside and the house had multiple kegs set up in various locations. The kind of party you love as a kid – and you hate as an adult if it is taking place in your neighborhood.

Being a new drinker, my tolerance level was non-existent and, for only the second time in my life I was thoroughly blasted (the first was at my brother Steve's wedding). However, my friend was driving me home and I knew that she was not drinking at all. I was being as responsible as a human being who could no longer form words could be.

She dropped me off and laughed as I became entangled in a tree while attempting to navigate the walkway to the front door of my home. I was especially quiet as I entered the house, went in the bathroom to get ready for bed and then continued down the hall to my bedroom, located right next to my parent's room.

Cold sweat started to bead up on my forehead and I could feel the bed swaying from side-to-side like one of those Viking boat rides at an amusement park. I rolled onto my back and dug the fingers of each hand into the side of the bed just wanting, praying for this perpetual motion to stop.

I was immediately aware that my insides were about to reject what I had put them through over the previous five hours so I quickly got out of bed and made my way down to the bathroom. I shut and locked the door behind me and proceeded to be sick. The cool tile floor of the bathroom felt good against my face as I lay by the base of the toilet, waiting on round two.

After my internal fireworks were complete, I meticulously cleaned everything that I could think of and, by the time I departed that bathroom, I was more than confident that there was not a trace of what had transpired in those early morning hours. I went back to bed and was out for the night.

The next morning I awoke to the smell of bacon wafting down the hall. I got up and followed my nose to the kitchen. Dad had already left for the day and Mom stood, in her green robe, with her back to me as she worked the frying pan.

"Good morning," I said raspily as I entered the kitchen in a wrinkled t-shirt and shorts.

"Good morning," she responded. "Are you hungry?"

"I am," I said. I was, and am, always hungry.

"Bacon and an English muffin sound good?" she asked.

"Perfect," I replied. Eggs were always an option but I thought, and think, eggs are nasty.

I poured myself a glass of orange juice and sat in Dad's seat, which was at the head of the kitchen table facing where Mom cooked. I looked out the bay window and silently cursed the sunlight that was pouring in over the table. For the first time in my life I felt a sympathetic connection to Bram Stroker's Dracula. I wondered if he wrote that book while battling a vicious hangover because the sun shining in through the window on my throbbing head felt like it had ignited a fuse which was going to make my brain explode.

"Did you have fun last night?" Mom asked.

"I did," I truthfully replied. "There were a lot of people from work. It was a good time."

There was a pause. "Were you drinking?" she asked without turning around.

Seconds felt like an hour. My brain rifled through scenarios that I desperately tried to piece together from the previous night. She knew something was up. I was sure I had perfectly cleaned that bathroom and I was fairly certain that I had remained silent through the process. I really just started drinking a few weeks prior to this incident and she had never questioned me before as to whether or not I was experimenting with alcohol.

"I wouldn't lie to you," I said getting ready to tell an aberration of the truth, "I had a couple." In my defense, it was sort of the truth, I did have a couple. I just left out the part that I then had about 20 more.

She turned, spatula gripped tightly in her right hand and with no love in her eyes. "Oh, I think you had more than a couple," she said icily.

I was dead in the water, my only play was on her emotions, "Mom, I never drank before, you know that. You also know I had a ride to and from the party from someone who, I swear to you, did not have a drop of alcohol," I explained. "Why don't you believe me when I said I only had a couple?"

She squared off on the other side of the kitchen island and stared right into my soul. "Because," she explained, "whenever it is 2:00 AM and someone crashes through my bedroom door and says, 'Mom, I'm hammered and I'm going to puke.' Then that same person slams my door shut and proceeds to stumble down the hall and gets sick for the rest of the night, I figure they've probably had more than a couple."

Well, I certainly had forgotten (forgotten sounds so much better than blacked-out) a rather important portion of the evening. I sat in silence as she brought my bacon and English muffin to the table and grabbed my empty glass to refill my orange juice.

"If your father hadn't fallen asleep in front of the television downstairs," she continued as she poured and brought me more juice, "you might not be alive this morning to reminisce about last night."

She never told him. Mom would get mad. Mom would lay down the law. Mom would strike the fear of God into you. Mom was not a rat.

I was dropped off another night after an evening of drinking. It was a Saturday and Don Kirchner's Rock Concert was just about to start. I went into the refrigerator and grabbed a plate of bacon and a quart sized jug of orange juice (I'm starting to see a theme).

I went to bed after consuming the bacon and orange juice. Sunday morning I was awoken with a loud banging on my door. "What," I growled into my pillow.

"Patrick," Mom barked through the closed door. "I need to talk to you."

"Uhhhhhhhhhhhhhh," I moaned. "Come in."

My door used to swell in the summer and would stick so I heard Mom crashing her closed fist into the top of my door three or four times before it finally swung in and smashed against the far wall.

"Did you eat bacon last night?" Mom asked as she came through the door.

"What?" I said, now looking in her direction but not being able to understand the urgency in which she needed to discuss my late night snacking habits.

"Bacon, Patrick," she said louder and distinctively clear, "Did YOU eat BACON when you came HOME LAST NIGHT?" Her speech was slow with the important words heavily, and loudly, emphasized like when you are speaking to someone who doesn't speak your language and you hope this method will magically allow them to understand.

My mind was finally coming out of a tired, drunken haze. I said, "Yes, Mom. I ate bacon last night. There was a plate of bacon and I ate it. I also had orange juice, if you care."

"There wasn't a plate of bacon, Patrick," she said with even more force than before. "There was a platter of bacon. A *platter* of bacon. A PLATTER of BACON." She held her hands out for me to have a decent visual on the approximate size of a platter. I remember thinking that if she just went downstairs the empty platter was probably still on the floor in front of the television.

I looked at her, now appreciating that the quantity of bacon that I had consumed might have been more than what I had previously assumed.

"Do you know how much bacon was on that platter, Patrick?" she asked. I didn't but I had a very good hint that I would momentarily. "Two pounds," she said. "You came home last night and ate two POUNDS of bacon."

She neither wanted nor needed an explanation. She turned and proceeded to walk down the hall saying to no one in particular, "I can't believe he just comes in the house and eats two pounds of bacon. Two pounds!"

I found out later that she had made all that bacon to go into something she was preparing that day for people who were coming to the house. Fortunately for her (and me) she was a wizard in the kitchen and could change an entire meal in a moment's notice. I did not feel it was in my best interest to pass along this compliment at that precise moment. I felt it best to just remain as silent and still as possible and hope that she would think nothing more of me than just another garbage disposal who would consume anything that was put in front of him.

As I let my head sink deeper into my pillow, I was overcome with a feeling of repulsion at the amount of bacon I consumed. However, that feeling began to dissolve, and I felt this strange pride swelling up inside of me. Two pounds. I ate two pounds of bacon.

Chapter 49

The circle remained formed around Dad on the porch. The temperature was comfortable and he was in the mood to talk.

"I took a look at a property next to a beautiful body of water," he said. This was not a hallucination, he had spoken of it before. "I think we could get 60 condominium units in that space. It would be a money-maker."

He slowly shook his head. "If I was younger I would do it. I can't take that type of risk now. If it didn't work for some reason, it would put your mother in a terrible position financially."

Two-days ago he was slumped over in a hospital bed, struggling to converse. Now he was thinking about developing properties.

And then, without warning or prodding, he completely shifted the conversation to sales and advertising. "I'm not sure why companies got away from jingles," he said. "They stick with you, forever. Politicians used to all have them for running for office. They worked."

He thought for a moment and then broke into songs about Pepsi Cola having 12 full ounces and ads for Dawson Beer. We were all thrown by this abrupt lesson in marketing and hearing these lyrics pulled from his memory banks.

He chuckled at having just sat here singing jingles from decades ago. "Anyway," he said, "if I can remember them now, well they must work."

He was getting tired. Everyone was getting tired by this point. We had been outside for over four hours and all agreed it was time to go in. As we were gathering up all of our items one other story popped into his head but it was back to when he was a Marine.

"I was on a battleship and there was a very high deck," he said. "No Marine would dive off of it, they kept talking like it would be great but no one would go first. Without saying anything, I walked back, put on my bathing suit and just started climbing up. People were all saying, look at McShane, he's going to do it. And I did. Then everyone did."

He smiled remembering the moment and continued, "It reminded me when I was little and I watched my father climb to the third landing of a diving platform. No one went to the third landing. The whole pool stopped and watched and he executed a beautiful swan dive."

A smile of great satisfaction and pride washed over his face.

Maura walked up behind him and began to wheel him back to his room where we were joined by Jim and Steve. He sat and ate his dinner. He was quieter now but smiled a lot and loved listening to stories about our lives.

Chapter 50

Any excuse to gather was enough to bring the McShanes together. Usually, gatherings would include whichever siblings were available to shoot down to Raynham Taunton Greyhound track, over to Dunn Gaherin's pub in Newton, or to grab a bite at The Chateau in Waltham.

The bigger gatherings were the best and they were almost always held at Mom and Dad's house in Weston. Everyone was there and the good-sized split-entry home was bursting with people coming and going. Laughter from the kitchen would only be drowned out by laughter from the living room. There was a constant fear of missing out regarding the conversations you couldn't be involved with because of the conversations in which you were actively engaged.

Being the seventh of the eight kids, I would actively view far more so than participate. Most often, in these gatherings, it was easier to just get caught up in the stories that were all around you rather than try to compete.

Holidays were the real reason to celebrate and we showed up en masse. Epic Easter egg hunts; Halloween costumes where Mom applied makeup as if we were just coming out of central casting; Thanksgiving with multiple tables, adults in the dining room, kids in the adjoining living room and a kitchen table covered with turkey, sides, pies and various desserts. The only constant was that Mom never sat for a moment. She just made constant laps with arms full of food.

Before every event Mom was a whirlwind cleaning the entire house with very little assistance. One of the more interesting household cleaners was the rug rake. For those who have never experienced the lush wonderment that was shag carpeting, the rug rake was an essential piece of cleaning apparatus.

It was a long pole with a flat piece of yellow plastic with thick plastic spikes (almost looked like mini-cones) protruding from the end. The yellow shag carpet that covered the upstairs of our home in the 1970s would regularly face the wrath of this device. Multiple times a day, Mom would be raking the foot prints out of the living room and hallway floor while dressed in a nice blouse and skirt, her hair and light makeup always done.

Joyce came home one day as Mom was feverishly raking the imprints from where Maura and I had been laying down in the living room playing a game of Sorry. She glanced in at Mom and said, "That's nice Mom. Where's Dad, vacuuming the lawn?"

Dad would stand in the kitchen, aggressively washing his hands in the sink, intently checking both sides to ensure they were thoroughly scrubbed. He was not a germaphobe but used to laugh about it saying that it must have been all those years on the oil truck that he just never felt his hands were clean.

I asked him if his father was the same with the constant cleansing. He thought for a moment and laughed. He said, "Now that you mention it, my Dad once said to me, 'Gerard, you sure do wash your hands a lot.' I guess it's just my thing."

Being such a large family, as the years passed, the siblings decided the cost was too great to purchase presents for each other so we implemented a Yankee swap. Everyone would buy a gift that was $20 in value or less, wrap it and put it in the middle of a pile. You would pick out the gift, unwrap it and then there was a whole elaborate switching game where randomly selected numbers would switch with one another. Some would try to find great bargains and have a nice gift in there, some would buy scratch tickets;

others would buy joke gifts. It was all done to provide the 30 or so participants an opportunity to sit in a circle in the living room and taunt each other.

Christmas evening, 1988, was the night I introduced my girlfriend, Theresa, who would become my wife, to my family. We had been dating for a mere five weeks. She was extremely nervous (terrified), not only at the sheer volume of immediate family members but at the wide disparity in ages. My oldest brothers and sister were very close in age to her parents.

Theresa was a little late arriving to our home. This trend has continued throughout her life. I think Theresa fell 20 minutes behind when she was five years old and has spent the rest of her life trying to catch up. She rang the doorbell as soon as we all formed a circle in the living room to begin the swap. Grins flickered across faces. I could only assume this was how the lions must have looked when the Romans were feeding them Christians.

I went down the flight of stairs and opened the front door. She stood there wearing a frozen smile that had nothing to do with the temperature. Theresa would be happiest if left unnoticed so she could slowly, and casually, blend into a scenario.

I took her coat to hang up. "Relax," I said reassuringly. "It's just my family."

Then, almost on cue, Joyce's voice rang out from somewhere in the living room. "Theresa, get up here and stand in the middle of this circle. We want to check you out." There was an explosion of laughter from the room. I laughed too and shrugged. "As I said," I repeated, "it's just my family. Good luck." Theresa met my family in the most in-your-face way imaginable. She was tossed into the deep end of the pool.

The night continued without too much focus on Theresa. While the humor can be merciless, the family also gave proper amounts of space and respect to allow someone to get acclimated. A couple of siblings that had younger children or that had obligations with their in-laws filtered out over the next couple of hours. As the crowd dwindled a bit, the remaining folks made their way to the dining room for poker. This was a nickel-and-dime, family game that was designed so no one could win or lose more than few dollars.

Theresa, who is a pretty good card player, was a very bad card player that night. She dug in to her purse a few times for additional funds. By the time the final cards flew that evening, she was out about $25, an astronomical amount of cash when factoring in the stakes and the limits.

Dad collected his winnings, he always won. He glanced up and said, "Thanks Pat, who are you bringing next week?"

Chapter 51

Maura and I said good-bye first and left for the restaurant. Mom, Jim and Steve would be meeting us shortly. Because Dad had esophagus problems, my parents stopped going to restaurants nearly a decade ago. This would be Mom's fourth time eating out in the past week and she loved every second of not having to prepare meals.

For this Mother's Day we wanted her to select where she most wanted to dine. She said she would love pizza. Cheap date.

Maura and I had not eaten in over 12 hours so when we arrived at the restaurant she immediately started looking at the appetizers. I went right to the desserts. She ordered spicy chicken. I ordered Ghirardeli Chocolate Chocolate Chip Ice Cream.

Mom, Steve and Jim arrived and found us devouring the first course.

"Sorry," I said. "We needed food."

"That's okay," Mom said. "Eat, eat."

The booth quickly filled with their bodies and Jim and Steve began pouring over the menus. Mom glanced around smiling. "Dad was great today, don't you think," she said. We all agreed.

"That was sad with Joyce and Mike, though," she continued.

We nodded. Not really wanting to go back to that moment. Mom has a tremendous gift for quickly pivoting in conversations. She is an optimist who always searches for the good in a situation.

"I thought everything ended up okay, though," she continued. "Dad's doing great and I think that he's going to be around for a quite a while longer."

There were murmurs of agreement from around the table. I smiled in her direction and nodded.

The waitress came back and we ordered another spicy chicken and an order of chicken teriyaki, along with a few pizzas for dinner.

We talked about everything except Dad while waiting for our food to be delivered. Everyone was pretty wiped out from the day, so there wasn't a normal McShane competition for conversation. Each time someone took the lead; everyone else leaned back and let them go, thankful that their only responsibility, at that instant, was to listen.

After fifteen minutes, the waitress returned with drink refills, our appetizers and small plates for everyone.

"Mom, try the spicy chicken," Steve said.

"Oh, I don't know if I'd like that," she said.

"I think you would," Maura said.

"Okay, but cut me off a tiny piece to try first," Mom said. "I really am just interested in the pizza."

We all sat at the table with drinks and plates covered with food. Mom had a glass of water in front of her and a small plate the size of a saucer that had 1/8 of a piece of spicy chicken and one sliver of celery.

The waitress walked by and gave a disturbed look as she glanced at the portions. Jim noticed this out of the corner of his eye, turned to Mom and said loudly enough for our waitress to hear, "Happy Mother's Day."

Chapter 52

Growing up, all who entered our house were welcomed with the crackling sound of a frying pan and were engulfed with the smell of beef. It was glorious. Your arteries would begin clogging just by ringing our door bell.

Breakfast was bacon, lunch was burgers and dinner was steak, or beef stew, or pot roast, or pork chops. Meat, meat, meat, meat. We did not eat salad for dinner; our meals ate salad for dinner.

On Saturday night we grabbed pizzas after Mass. Unless it was Lent, then pizza got moved to Friday and meat made a return to the Saturday night lineup. On Wednesdays we had spaghetti because in Boston, the Prince Spaghetti Company had a commercial with a boy named Anthony who would run through the streets of the North End as his mother leaned out the window calling, "Anthony! Anthony!" The Irish got the message that Wednesday was Prince Spaghetti day (with meat sauce).

Mom always had her back to the kitchen door as she adeptly managed at least two frying pans and numerous trays in the oven. She would turn, address you by name and offer up what she was cooking.

"Patrick, are you in the mood for a hamburger?" Nothing remarkable there, I agree. It was the next line that I never fully appreciated as a kid. "Or do you want something else? What are you in the mood for?"

What are you in the mood for? Think about that for a second. There were my parents and eight kids and she's asking people what they want like she's working at a diner.

It was not uncommon to see three or four completely different meals at the same time. Special orders always welcome. Mom once made me three dinners because I had no idea what I wanted. She made me a steak and French fries, a chicken pot pie and a Stouffer's French Bread Pizza. She said, "Just have a little of each." I had a lot of each. Okay, I had all of each.

If I was working a night shift, Mom would call me and say, "Are you coming home after work?"

If the answer was yes she would say, "What time?"

"About 10 o'clock."

"Do you want something to eat?"

There were no boundaries. I could say yes, French Toast; steak; lasagna. You name it. If the ingredients were in the house and she had enough time, that's what you would be having for dinner.

For an Irish lady, Mom crammed food into you like an Italian. She always enjoyed people devouring what she made and would assist in continuing to fill up your plate as soon as you were wrapping up the first course. She would normally start shoveling out huge portions of desserts. These would appear before you with the statement, "Of course you are going to have some dessert."

Dad would sit at the far end of the rectangular kitchen table facing Mom. The Boston Globe was always folded neatly in front of him. With his glasses perched on his nose he would begin by reading the Sports section, then he would read business, the front section, Metro/Region and completely skip Arts and Entertainment. When Mom sat down she would read the front section, Metro Region, Business, the books section of Arts and Entertainment and glance at the Sports page. She was conversant at sports for much of her life but as the kids grew and moved out of the house, she became nearly as passionate as Dad about the Boston teams.

Mom made delicious meals but that's not what I remember. Meal time was a constant flow of family and conversation. We lived in Weston, Massachusetts and for a long time all the siblings lived within 30 minutes of home. Two of my brothers were police officers in our town. Jim was Chief and Steve was a patrolman.

On the weekends it was steady. Not coordinated. No one ever had to call to say they were thinking about coming by. Of course you were coming by. There is no place else we would rather be.

"Oh, you just missed Marsha," or "Ed's going to be swinging by after the BC game." The kitchen in my parents' home was the center of our universe.

You just had to understand the boundaries. Mom was always available for a conversation. Dad was available most of the time, unless the Patriots, Red Sox, Celtics, Boston College or Notre Dame was on. Then he was downstairs sitting in his chair and you were more than welcome to watch with him. However, conversation was limited to the most recently completed play. And that conversation needed to be done quickly because he wanted to hear what the analysts had to say.

Mom and Dad were never hard to find. They were home, at Mass or at the Natick Mall. Their social circle consisted of family. They created a bunch of people they liked and said, "this is who we'll hang out with." Mom was a stay-at-home and Dad never had a job where he traveled. There was always conversation, laughter and political debate.

We weren't a Norman Rockwell painting of a family gathered around a table. If there was a game on, meals would be brought downstairs in front of the television. Meal time was not a designated time. You ate when you were hungry. We were NEVER forced to eat something we did not like. That always seemed petty and ridiculous.

It was not uncommon to have a few people sitting around a table, someone else standing at the kitchen counter, and someone leaning over the sink, gulping down a sandwich before having to run out. It was part of the fun, there were always people coming and going.

You could sit at the kitchen table for hours and be thoroughly entertained. Dad would be in his seat, Mom would be firing off meal after meal and the kids and grandkids would be dropping by, funneling through, each with their own stories.

Meal time was delicious for all the senses.

Chapter 53

Maura and I drove Mom home after eating.

Mom was simultaneously enthusiastic and exhausted. She sat in the back seat, head held high and staring out the window. She showed signs of being tired, with her left arm supporting her body weight as it rested on the arm rest on the door. Her right arm casually hung by her side.

I thought of what she must be feeling. How can this not be mentally tearing her apart each and every moment? They were the other half of each other after all these years.

"He was really good today," she said casually not really to anyone in particular. "I couldn't believe some of the stories that he was coming up with."

"I know," Maura replied. "I had never heard some of those."

"Oh yeah, he's told them but some I haven't heard in decades," Mom said. "When everyone got around him it was like something sparked. He just kept coming up with all these things."

"How is he when it's just the two of you?" I asked.

"Before you kids came down?" She said.

"Yeah."

"Well," Mom paused a bit, "well he wasn't good. He was so worn out and just seemed exhausted. It seemed like the end was coming. Not like he was giving up, just more like he didn't have the power to do it anymore."

It was a beautiful night and I was just staring at trees as we buzzed by them. I was out of words.

"But then you kids came and he is charged up again," she smiled and nodded. "We might have to move all of you down here to keep him going."

There was an elderly couple walking down the sidewalk together as Mom spoke. She was carrying a purse clutched tightly in her right hand. He was carrying a plastic bag of groceries in his right hand. She walked a half pace in front of him.

I couldn't help but think of how many times Mom and Dad did this exact same walk and, no matter how well Dad seemed now, the days of them walking together outside were over. For as well as Dad was doing the last couple of days, he was always either in a bed or in a wheelchair and no prognosis had him being able to get back on his feet for long (or even short) walks.

"You know I think he looked really good too," Mom continued.

"Yes, he definitely did.," Maura confirmed.

Mom glanced over at me. "Pat, you're being quiet."

"I'm good," I said defensively. "Just a little worn down from the day, I guess."

"Yeah, it was a long day," Mom agreed. "But a good day. A great day."

I nodded.

"You kids coming down have made such a difference in him," Mom said.

"It's amazing," Maura chimed in as she pulled into Mom's condo complex. "He is a different person than he was just a couple of days ago."

As Maura pulled into the parking spot I absolutely understood that this was not just hyperbole. He was an entirely different person than who I saw when we walked into that hospital for the first time.

I got out of the car and helped Mom out. She and Maura said their good byes and Mom and I walked up the winding path into her complex. She was very casual in how she spoke as we waited for the elevator but my eyes were fixed out the glass door that led to the covered parking garage. Mom and Dad own the first spot by the door. It sat empty. I couldn't help think that his car should be there, not sitting in my garage in Massachusetts.

The elevator opened and we got on. I thought of my Mother from this point forward making this journey into her home by herself. Mom kept chatting.

We walked to her condo and I gave her a hug good night and said I would see her in the morning. She thanked me again. I waited as she put the key in the lock and opened her door. She turned back to me and smiled and said, "I guess this is it, have a good night!"

I smiled and said, "Good night." And then I watched her walk into her condo.

Alone.

Chapter 54

While attending college where Dad worked was nothing like the movie Back to School starring Rodney Dangerfield, I quickly realized that he was one of the main reasons why I was able to connect with students so quickly. He was beloved by students, professors and employees. He was the person people wanted to be around and I was riding his coattails.

I would regularly go to the gym to shoot baskets and speak with him. There were times where I would vent about classes that I was in; there were times when I just needed to talk.

Sophomore year was a disaster. I don't know if it was me or the classes but everything I touched went sour. I was put on academic probation and desperately fought to remain a student. Dad knew some really intelligent athletes at the school and was able to line me up with tremendous tutors.

In financial accounting I needed a 66 on the final to pass the class. I told Dad, and anyone that would listen, that if I didn't get a passing grade I was done with Bentley. I just could not grasp that class. Dad was supportive of my plight but forceful in his direction. "Pass the class. Remember, you are getting a free ride."

On the night the grades were posted on the professor's door, I walked over to the dimly lit, silent and empty building that housed the professors offices. I made my way down the hall and stopped outside of my accounting professor's door. I placed a hand over the final grades of the exam and found my student ID number. I squeezed the first number of my grade. "6." This second number was going to determine my future. I slowly slid my hand to the right. "6."

I let out a bellowing, "YEAAAAAAAAAAAAAAAAAAHHHHHH" and proceeded to throw three consecutive punches into my professor's door. Left…bam!…Right…bam!…Left…bam!

The spontaneous celebration was met with an immediate response. My professor who, unbeknownst to me, was in his office screamed. "Open that door now!"

My heart sank. I thought about making a break for it. He would never know it was me. Instead, I slowly and sheepishly opened the door. My professor sat at his desk. Eyes glaring at me through gold wire-rimmed glasses. Another man sat across the desk from him. Neither said anything. They both stared.

"Ssssorry," I stammered, "I, I didn't realize…"

He spoke quickly, cutting me off. "Did you get one of the four As?" he asked.

I didn't even comprehend what he was saying. All I could say was, "Excuse me?"

"One of the four As," he repeated. "Out of the 126 students in this class I awarded four As. Were you one of those four?"

He obviously had no idea who I was and, for the first time in this exchange a grin began a slow but unyielding creep across my face. "No sir, I did not."

He smiled. He looked across the desk at his companion. Turning back to me he said, "You got a D didn't you?"

Ding, ding, ding. We have a winner.

"Yes, I did," I said embarrassed and slightly laughing at the same time.

A wide smile crossed his face as he leaned back and said, "Nice job." He then turned back to the gentleman he was meeting with and said, "You only get that reaction from the As and Ds."

He looked back to me and said, "Congratulations. Go celebrate."

My celebration was jumping in my car and driving over to the gym to tell Dad that I made it over that mountain. There were tens of thousands of tuition dollar smiles that beamed out of his office that night.

Chapter 55

Steve, Maura, Maura's fiancé Tim and her daughter Jacquelyn sat in Maura's living room talking about everything that would need to happen. Jim was outside talking to one of his kids.

"There is so much to think about," Maura said. "If anything happens, so much has to happen so fast."

I called out from the kitchen to enter into the conversation, "Hey Maura, tell Steve what Mom said to you about funeral planning," I urged. I quickly walked back into the room to see Steve's reaction.

"Oh," Maura said matter-of-factly, "she was coming up with a plan on who to assign tasks to if anything happened. She was just rattling them off: Joyce would have to pick out the linen for inside the coffin, but it has to be white; Jim could research hotel costs in the Natick area and there were a few others. Then she turned to me and said, I may need you to pull the plug."

I had already heard the story but we all started laughing. Not sure if that was a position of honor or not but everyone, except Maura, was thrilled that was her appointed role.

"Well, one of the eight needed the rest of their life ruined," I said, "may as well be you."

"The benefits of living close by," Maura said.

"Well, just let us know how we can help," Steve said. "With the service and burial taking place up in Massachusetts, we can do a lot up there."

"There is one thing that we will definitely need help with," Maura said.

She looked at me.

"The obituary," she said. "There is no way Mom is going to be able to do that with everything else that is going to be happening."

"No worries," I said. "I'll do it."

"That would be huge," Maura said.

"If you like," I said, "I could put one together for you guys to review and we would be all set in case anything happens."

"Put down ideas," Steve said, "but don't write his obituary."

I looked up at Steve and smiled. "Do you really think if I write an obituary for Dad it's going to cause him to die sooner?"

Steve didn't say anything but he did look uncomfortable.

"You think I have that kind of power?" I continued. "Because I'll tell you what, if I was blessed with that ability, there would be about 5 to 10 obits I'd be knocking out before turning in for bed tonight."

Steve, Maura and Jacquelyn laughed.

Steve said, "Fine, but not Dad's."

"Okay."

It was late and we all dispersed to get ready for bed. As I waited for my turn in the bathroom I laid on the bed, looking up at the ceiling. This visit had gone so fast. I thought of Joyce and Mike from earlier today and their good-bye. I knew that it was my turn to say good-bye tomorrow.

Jim walked over to where I was laying down. He said "Steve and I are going to take off and give you time alone with Dad tomorrow."

"Thanks, I appreciate it," I said.

"You know, Patrick," he continued, "the way he's been, I'm just telling myself that I'm going to come back down in a couple of months and will see him again."

"Yeah," I said. "I think I'm going to try and do the same."

"It's not a lie," he said, "I really think he's going to be around for a while."

Jim turned and walked back to where his bed was. I closed my eyes and wondered if I could tell myself that too. If, when the time came to say goodbye, if I would really believe that I would see him again.

Chapter 56

Dad's disdain for alcohol may have only been surpassed for his unforgiving intolerance of vulgarity, especially if used in front of women. He was in no way a prude but he was raised to treat people with respect and he demanded that from himself and from each one of his children.

After my oldest daughter Jillian's baptism we had each side of the family gather at my in-law's house for the celebration. Theresa and I lived in a little, one-bedroom condominium that would be busting at the seams with 20 people, and we had about 80 in attendance.

As I was standing by the trays of food speaking with my Dad, my wife's cousin came by. He is a great, funny guy whom we spent a lot of time with as young couples. I grabbed his arm as he was passing and made a quick introduction to Dad.

Dad reached his right hand out smiled and said, "It's nice meeting you."

With hands locked in the shake and staring into each other's eyes the sentence that will live with me forever came out of Theresa's cousin's mouth. He said, "Mr. McShane, it's a pleasure meeting you. And let me tell you, you wouldn't believe how many times your son has gotten me fucking shit-faced."

Dad did not release his grip; he just slowly turned his head to face me. All life had seeped out of my body. I mouthed, "I don't know." Not even sure what I was trying to communicate there, just maybe that I don't know what I could possibly do with that sentence. Dad gave a half sigh and just turned. The moment was never discussed.

To drive home how horrific that sentence must have been to my Dad's ears, those words were not only never said in my house, they were never even in consideration to be said. Little side-filler curse words like "crap" or "damn" were in no way tolerated in my home growing-up.

Mom and Dad used to go to New York every year for a mini-vacation. One year they went to see Oklahoma on Broadway. In the early part of the show the lead singer sang, "My boy Bill is a little bastard…" Dad nudged Mom with a soft elbow and said, "Let's go." They got up and walked out. He would not tolerate bad language being used in front of women in any forum, including in the play Oklahoma on Broadway.

When Dad was driving the McShane Oil truck as a younger man, he used to stop at various diners to eat. Mom told me he had a favorite diner and on multiple occasions he told truck drivers to watch their language because there was a woman present, referring to the waitress.

One day he walked into the diner and sat down. The waitress had her back turned and did not see him enter. She let out a string of profanities describing something. She turned and saw him sitting in a booth. She said, "Oh, Gerard, I'm so sorry I had no idea that you had come in." Without speaking he shook his head, got up and left.

Dad stressed showing respect for others, taking care of those who might not be in a position to take care of themselves and, above all else, carrying yourself with dignity. At that moment, he realized that he was fighting for her dignity and respect more than she was. He felt disappointed and foolish. He would do whatever he could for you until you made him look foolish and then you were dead to him. He never returned to that diner.

There was a time when I was 14 that my parents were sitting at opposite ends of the kitchen table and I was getting some cookies (I would like to say this was a daily occasion but it was more of an hourly event). I distinctly remember dropping two of the cookies on the ground and saying, "What the hell…"

As soon as the words left my mouth, I froze. Mom turned in her seat and looked at me and gave a small laugh. Dad lowered the newspaper to the table and looked at me.

"Sorry," I said sheepishly.

"Watch your language," he said.

"You can tell that was a mistake, Gerard," Mom said.

"I can tell that sentence flowed pretty smoothly," Dad responded still looking at me. "Like it's said on a regular basis. Not in this house."

"Understood," I said. And I did understand and he was right. That sentence did flow easily because it is one swear that I did say outside of the home and with my friends. The reason I said it was mainly because I would get my chops busted on a fairly regular basis because I never swore. It was my go-to swear sentence.

Yup. "What the hell" was my way of being a rebel at the age of 14. Strict parenting - I'm telling you, it works.

Around that same time my sister Marsha had a boyfriend over to the house for a family gathering. Marsha was in her thirties and her boyfriend was in his forties. As with most parties, the majority of people were gathered in the kitchen. Dad sitting in the seat he always occupied.

Marsha looked at her boyfriend and reminded him that they had to leave as they were going to another party. He glanced up at the clock and said, "Hey, as Bobby Orr would say, let's get the puck out of here."

One by one people drifted out of each of the three exits in that room, leaving just Marsha and her boyfriend alone with Dad. He didn't say anything about it but it was just uncomfortable enough to be remembered for years.

As my sister's boyfriend walked past many of us siblings standing next to each other in the hall laughing, he sarcastically thanked each of us for our support before leaving. He pulled the pin on that grenade; no reason why we were going to jump on it to save him.

Ten years after my parents sold McShane Oil, I was driving behind one of the trucks in Waltham on my way to class at Bentley College. As I waited at a red light, a driver blew through a light to cut off the McShane Oil truck driver.

The driver who blew through the light had nowhere to go as he was immediately in stopped traffic. The driver of the McShane Oil truck proceeded to lean out the window and let loose a stream of profanities that would make a longshoreman blush. I was infuriated. I saw my name, more importantly, my father's name being represented in a way that was entirely contrary to all that he had espoused.

Upon arriving at campus, I took a right to drive down the hill to the gym where Dad worked instead of taking a left and driving up the hill to my class. I jumped out of my car and made a beeline to Dad's office. He was sitting behind his desk and glanced up at me as I walked through the door.

"I want to buy McShane Oil back," I said.

"Not me," he replied.

I then explained to him what I had just experienced.

"It's not ours anymore," he calmly said.

"It's our name," I said with more than a hint of exasperation. I knew that we couldn't just take the business back but I think I wanted to see the anger coming out of him.

"I don't like it any more than you do," he said. "Actually, I'm pretty sure that it bothers me more than you but they bought the business and the business name. I don't know who they have driving for them and it doesn't really matter. They have to run their business as they best see fit. We can only control ourselves."

I still wasn't happy but it was interesting to see a man that now had more of an introspective viewpoint on life than what I had seen in my years growing up.

"Don't you have class?" he said breaking the silence.

"Yeah," I said.

"Well, go to class," he said.

Throughout my college years he was my sense of normalcy and sanity on that campus. I remember sharing and laughing more with him than anyone else at that school over those years.

Dad's resignation/retirement notice coincided with my graduation – he told me he wanted to be out two years prior but he was not going to give up that free tuition. I'm sure there were many people who wished that I went on the five year plan to keep him around a while longer.

At his retirement party (which he had no use for as he truly did not embrace large social gatherings, especially those that were centered on him) he was presented with a Bentley College rocking chair that was a memento and also a dig at his advanced age.

That chair sits in my house to this day.

Chapter 57

Jim and Steve were talking over breakfast as I finished packing. "I'm all set," I said.

We went out front and jumped in the car. I sat in back and looked out the window at corner after corner of Publix Super Markets, CVS' and Hess Stations. While I was trying to convince myself that there was no reason to believe that I would not see Dad again, I also very much thought that this would be the last time I ever saw him.

"We're going to let you have time alone with Dad today," Steve said.

"I told him," Jim said.

"Yeah, thanks," I said.

Usually there was a lot of talking and joking on our rides. Today's ride was different. It was filled with large collections of silence. Uncomfortable silence.

"I hope he's good today for you," Steve said.

"Me too," I said. "But I'm okay if he's not. We got a whole lot more than I thought we were going to get."

"And no one can ever take this away from us," Jim added. "This time with Dad, the joking, the stories, being down here to watch the Derby with him. This couldn't have been any better."

"It's been amazing," I said and looked back out the window, this time at rows of senior living complexes, occasionally punctuated by the all too familiar CVS, Publix market and Hess station. "I told Maura that her email was the best thing she could have sent out. It lit a fire under us and we had a perfect visit."

"I think she felt bad," Steve said. "I think she felt that she got us down here thinking that this was the end and it may not be and maybe we would have preferred coming down a little later."

Jim was shaking his head, "This couldn't have been any better."

"I told her," I said, "that she could not have gotten us down here at a better time. I told her that we got to talk and laugh with him and he knows who we are."

"He doesn't know my name," Steve said, "The Other One."

"I told her that I would so far prefer this to being here at the very end if he was just lying in a bed, unable to converse, not realizing that we are even at his bedside," I said.

"I don't need to be at his bedside at the end," I said aloud to them and to convince myself. "I think it is so much better that we were here now."

We pulled in to the skilled nursing facility and parked. The three of us walked into the building and took a right and went down the hall. Residents in wheelchairs lined hallways, smiled and said good morning. We were regulars.

We took a right at the end of the hall and there was Dad, sitting in his wheelchair, dressed and ready for the day's activities.

"What are you doing out here Dad?" Jim asked.

"I don't know," he said.

"Did you have breakfast?" Jim said.

"Yes," he said.

He did not seem as connected this morning. He was clutching and folding a piece of Kleenex and not very talkative.

"Do you want to go outside?" Steve asked, obviously trying to capture some of the magic from the last couple of days."

"I don't know," he said.

"It's beautiful out there," I said. "Nice day to be outside."

"Yeah, Dad, take advantage of these days before it gets really hot," Jim added.

"Okay," Dad said. "Let's go."

Steve got behind to wheel him out and Jim and I led the way. We brought him back out onto the patio where we sat for so long yesterday. We pulled three chairs up to his wheelchair.

Chapter 58

The house I grew up in was situated on the corner of Country Drive and Surrey Lane in Weston, Massachusetts. It was a white, split entry home with black shutters. There was a two car garage under my bedroom and Mom and Dad's bedroom.

The house sat on two wooded acres of land. The family who owned the home prior to our purchase loved those woods so much they built a giant boardwalk that was in the shape of a diamond that went throughout the property and allowed you to walk over some of the streams and wetlands.

As a child it was a great place to escape, to just walk the property or meet friends at designated spots on the boardwalk. Mom and Dad, or any other adult, almost never went back on them - unless there was a purpose or a suspicion. This made for a wonderland for kids to just get away.

From various spots in the woods, there was a clear view of the back of our house and the sliding glass door that went into our TV room. On occasion, the door would slide open and Mom or Dad would walk out and their eyes would scan the woods. I would watch, knowing that they were trying see if I was back there but, sometimes, you just needed to be left alone.

"Pat," a voice would call into the woods. I'd sit motionless.

"Pat," the voice would repeat. You could tell by the tone of the voice the urgency of the call of your name. If it was merely for a question or conversation, there was no need to respond. I could see them turn and walk back into the house, sliding the door shut behind them.

The joys of a pre-cell phone connected life. Out of sight, out of contact.

Jim originally gave Dad a heads-up regarding the Country Drive house. Dad would buy and sell houses often, always moving up a little and gaining a little more space for the family. Dad said that it sounded like something he would be interested in and he drove over and took a look. A few hours later Jim's phone rang. Dad said that he took a look but it just was not the right style for his taste.

Jim was confused, it seemed to have the space and exact style that Dad wanted. Being on the police force, Jim would drive past the house every day and was amazed at how many people must have agreed with Dad because the house just sat, with no buyers.

Many months later, Jim casually mentioned that the house was still for sale to Dad. Dad looked quizzically at him and said, "The house you told me to see sold shortly after I looked at it." Jim shook his head and assured him that it was still for sale.

Dad had looked at the wrong house.

He and a friend (the investor, back when they were still on speaking terms) were looking at a number of properties that weekend. Dad, without thinking, said they should go and take a look at this house too. As the car took a left off of Surrey Lane and turned onto Country Drive both men exclaimed, "I want it."

Dad pulled into the driveway and parked right outside the garage. This was not the house he had already seen and now he brought a competitive bidder to the property in his own car!

Before walking in, he turned and said, "Look, there's no reason for us to fight each other for this house. It will just end up costing one of us a lot of money." He pulled a coin from his pocket and gingerly rolled it between his thumb and fore-fingers. "You agree?"

His friend nodded. Dad flipped the coin into the air, it spun side over side.

"Tails," his friend said with authority.

Dad caught the coin in his right hand and slapped it down on the back of his left hand. He and his friend exchanged grins as he slowly uncovered the coin. It was heads. Without walking in, he knew he would buy this house.

The inside was repugnant. Food stuck to the counters and cabinets. Walls destroyed with graffiti, and bathrooms appeared to have last been cleaned a few calendars ago. When Dad brought Mom over he pleaded with her to look past all the filth and clutter. He knew that, without this glorious mess, his gaffe of looking at the wrong house months ago would have surely cost us this home.

That was our house for twenty years. It sat at the heart of a great neighborhood which provided us friends and extended families that would last a lifetime. But even more than the external, the house was the central meeting place for all the kids and their families.

Christmas was the holiday we all loved the most. Our tree stood in the corner of the living room with the stockings hung casually in front of the chimney on the other side of the room. Mom and Dad did not over-decorate but there was plenty of Christmas bling in each room. Cards that were sent to our family covered the piano, doorways and counter spaces.

The real joy was when we all came back together. Everyone crammed into that living room to share stories and jokes. Dad would sit in the yellow easy chair by the dining room and Mom would be on the end of the couch. Continuous laughter would ricochet off those walls. When I close my eyes, I still see Dad with his left leg crossed over his right knee, laughing, his hand coming down to slap his right thigh. You knew you cracked Dad up when that right hand hit that right thigh.

In 1992 my parents decided to sell the house and split their time between a townhouse in Dedham and an apartment in Florida while deciding where they were finally going to settle. For two people who always preached to never become attached to objects, they (and we) were crushed at the thought that this house would no longer be in our lives.

It was more than a property. It was where we saw each other. It was where we spent time with Mom and Dad. It was where we celebrated every major life event for the last 20 years. And now it was going to be gone.

I drove to the Weston house the day my parents were packing up the Buick with the last remnants of the house. Steve and Ed were there as well. The five of us stood in the driveway talking. The Buick was packed so tight with objects that Mom would have to lean forward for the entire ride to Florida.

"Mom, I really don't think that you are going to be able to ride all the way to Florida like that," Ed said.

She glanced at the seat and shook her head, "This is nothing. I'll be fine."

"Your back, Ma," replied Steve. "You'll be leaning into the windshield the whole way to Florida."

She shook her head with a tight grin, "It's nothing. I like sitting straight up. It's good for the posture."

Never a complaint. Ever. Mom and Dad took what life gave them and were happy to have it. They were fortunate and grateful but also never expected much. Life was good to them. They felt that nobody owed them anything.

Mom hugged us good-bye, Dad shook our hands. They got in the car. Mom could not have been comfortable but she was smiling. They backed out of the driveway. We walked toward the car. Their car angled out and they each waved to us. They then slowly started to pull away; I noticed a slight pause as Dad pumped the breaks as they passed the house. Dad then stepped heavier on the gas and we watched as their car turned onto Surrey Lane and caught glimpses of the vehicle through the trees as it, and they, drove away.

We turned back to the house and didn't say much of anything. A chapter had ended. A really good chapter.

Chapter 59

The patio out front was wide open this day. Not a person in sight and the weather was, once again, absolutely perfect. Dad on the other hand appeared to be a bit more agitated and not being able to get comfortable.

"Move that chair," Dad said motioning to a chair that was situated to his left and was soon to be occupied by me.

I went over and picked it up. "Where do you want it?"

"Over a bit, out of the sun," he said. He pointed a couple of steps in closer, which caused everyone else to shift as I would now be occupying the center of our newly formed circle.

I shifted it.

"More," he said.

I shifted it some more.

"Good," he said.

His fingers fidgeted like he was looking for something.

"Do you want something, Dad?" Steve asked.

"No," he said.

"Do you want a Kleenex?" Steve said.

"Yeah," Dad said.

Jim got up and said that he would go grab a box and be right back.

Steve cracked a couple of jokes but Dad only gave small grins. He wasn't participating right now so the conversation was at a minimum. His eyes would glance off to the left at the parking lot. Any activity or movement was drawing his attention away from us.

Jim popped back out from the door. "Dad, the therapist was looking for you," he said. "We have to get you back in there."

"Okay," Dad said. Not really engaged with us or seemingly caring where he needed to be at that moment.

Jim was pushing Dad's wheelchair and Steve was leading the way.

Jim laughed and said to me in a hushed voice, "They said they got him ready to go to therapy and then he was gone."

That's life when you're dealing with sons. Dad is all dressed, fed, cleaned and in a wheelchair in the hallway, never even crossed our mind that someone else might have an agenda other than the one we had for ourselves.

The therapist greeted us right outside of Dad's room.

"There you are," she said with a smile in Dad's direction. "We've been looking all over for you." She stared at him. The message was for us.

"How long will he be in therapy?" Steve asked.

"We'll have him back to his room in about an hour," she said.

Jim and Steve were quiet. "Okay," I said. "That's great."

She walked away with Dad.

"I'm fine," I said knowing that they both felt terrible because this was my last day with him.

"It just stinks that they pick now to do the therapy," Jim said. "We could see if they could reschedule for this afternoon."

"He'll be back by 11:30," I said. "I don't have to leave until 2:00."

"Well, we'll go get Ma at 11:30 but will hang out with her at the condo. It will still give you alone time for a little bit," Steve said.

"It's fine," I repeated.

"And when we bring Ma back," Jim continued, "we'll take off and grab lunch and just meet you back in the lobby by the receptionist at 2:00 PM. That'll give you time with just Ma and Dad."

"Perfect," I said. "Thank you."

"No sense standing around here," Jim said, "Let's go over to Dunks."

We drove to Dunks. Coffee. Coffee. Hot chocolate with whipped cream. We sat inside today, at a small table up against a wall.

"It's lousy that your time is getting cut into," Steve said. He and Jim were clearly more agitated with the situation that I was. It was unfortunate but with still no idea what I was supposed to say or how I was supposed to say it, two hours seemed like more than enough time to me.

"I'm really fine with it," I said. "We got so much more than I ever imagined we would. Hey, when we were flying down here, I thought he might not still be around today."

Steve looked towards the window as Jim's eyes focused more on the ground. They both slightly nodded their agreement.

Chapter 60

When my parents decided to settle in Florida in 1994 they were faced with an odd and unexpected situation. Because of the ways the tax laws were written at the time, Mom and Dad had to roll at least two-thirds of the sale price of their Weston home into the purchase price of a new home. They also had to occupy the new home for at least two years before selling.

When you are selling a house in Weston, Massachusetts and only wanting to buy a condominium in the Tampa, Florida region, it creates quite a conundrum. Specifically, they had to pay about six times more for a condo than what they wanted to purchase.

Mom and Dad never made a show over how financially comfortable they may have been. If you really look at their lives, Dad never really had a high-paying job and Mom had not collected a paycheck since she was 21 AND there were eight of us kids. Their relative strong financial position never made a lot of sense on first glance and the best way I can describe it is that they bought Hood ice cream.

Mom and Dad's favorite kind of ice cream was Brigham's. They liked Hood and thought it was very good but it did not quite have the flavor of Brigham's. They had the money to buy Brigham's. They had enough money to buy as much Brigham's ice cream as they could eat. However, Hood generally cost about one third less than Brigham's. Now, take that philosophy and apply it to every aspect of your life. The next thing you know, you amass an impressive net-worth.

They were not frugal by any sense of the imagination. They were two of the most generous people I've ever encountered with their money. It was just a mindset that they did not need to continually consume what they liked the most, it was perfectly fine to live beneath your means and consume items that you liked but were not necessarily your ideal.

They were Depression-era kids and this behavior was a necessity. As children and young adults they did not have the money to afford the items that they really wanted so they learned to be happy with what they could work into their budget. As years passed, and their savings grew, they kept the same mentality of always living well within their means.

"We're happy," Mom once explained to me, "we don't feel the need to try and impress anybody with objects."

But now here they were, faced with the tax necessity to move to a private, gated community in Tampa, Florida called Harbor Island. This is where the haves were overjoyed to have the private gate lowered to not allow the have-nots entrance. It was everything Mom and Dad were not.

It was, however, near Maura and the price point was right on target with what they were required to spend. Mom and Dad drove over to look at a two story sprawling, 2,200 square foot condominium that had balconies on two floors that overlooked a private inlet.

Dad was driving my old Chevy Chevette. He took it to get the last ounce of life out if it before they traded it in on a new car…which was a mere few days away from happening. Somewhere after being let in the private gate and before making it to the sales office, the car died.

"You've got to be kidding me," Dad said.

"What?" Mom replied. "What's going on?"

"It's dead." Dad said as he pulled to the side of the road. He saw the sales office was up ahead.

"Hop out," he said to Mom.

She got out and he instructed her to sit in the drivers seat.

"Put it in drive," he said laughing to himself as he pushed the Chevette into the parking lot of the sales office and next to a Mercedes and an Audi.

"They must be looking thinking they got a couple of winners here," Dad said to Mom as she stepped out of the car.

They toured and loved everything about the condominium.

The listing broker, who was employed by the development, told Mom and Dad that, unfortunately, this was one was verbally committed to this morning but they were hoping to have another one that was inland come available in the next two weeks.

Dad had been around the block a couple of thousand times and knew that there was always "a buyer who was coming in this afternoon so you better hurry."

"You don't have a signed agreement?"

The broker shook her head but quickly added, "No but the gentleman who is taking this will be quite exciting to have at the community."

Dad still had no idea if this was fiction or non-fiction. He did, however, know that he wanted this condominium. It checked all the boxes. He paused and watched her for a while. Waiting for her to say something with which he could work.

"I shouldn't say this," she excitedly began, "but do you want to know who it is?"

Neither Mom or Dad cared a bit about celebrity. Dad began to shake his head no. Mom politely engaged, "Yes, who is it?"

"Norman Schwarzkopf!" She said with excitement.

That caught Dad's attention. While Dad recognized the leadership, bravery and military excellence of General Schwarzkopf, he had grown frustrated by a few recent interviews the General had done where he had seemed to disregard the intelligence of those who worked alongside him. Dad thought he sounded pretentious and self-serving.

In short, Dad thought it would be funny to take him down a notch.

Dad made an offer on the spot for the condominium. "I really can't," the broker said.

"You don't have signed agreement," Dad replied. "Can you tell me if my offer is better than the one he submitted?"

"Well, it's different," she responded.

"What do you mean?"

"Well," she continued, "his is a rental offer."

"The owner wants to rent?"

"His offer is to rent for a year and then if he likes it he will buy."

"You need to take my offer to the seller," Dad said. "I'm sure when given the opportunity, the seller will want the cash."

Mom and Dad got the condo.

Chapter 61

We headed back over to the skilled nursing facility and made our way down to Dad's room.

He was seated in his wheelchair next to his bed, wearing plaid sweat pants, his gray sweater and his Red Sox cap. They had just brought him lunch. I stood on the opposite side of his bed and Jim and Steve stood at the foot of his bed.

"Dad," Jim said. "Steve and I have to go get Ma but Pat's going to stay here with you."

"Okay," Dad said.

Steve motioned for me to come out from the side of the bed. He picked up the bed and shifted the base a couple of feet to the left so I could get in and sit next to Dad. Jim and Steve took off as I positioned myself where we were at a comfortable speaking distance but also where I could provide assistance in case it was needed.

He had chopped chicken, mashed potatoes, beets and a dessert. While he was not expressing any level of anxiety it was clear his frustrations were growing as he was having continued difficulties managing his utensils.

"Let me give you a hand," I said and picked up the fork and fed him. He didn't want anything to do with the meat but really liked the potatoes (smothered in butter) and would tolerate the beets.

He would take a bite and sit back as if to rest. In the down moments, I was working on gathering more information to store away in my memory. "If I wanted to show my girls one Marx Brothers movie," I said, "what would it be?"

"That's easy," he said, "A Night at the Opera."

I tried to feed him some more beets and mashed potatoes but he shook his head no.

"How about the dessert?" I said.

"Yeah, okay," he responded.

I shifted the plates, "Looks like apple pie," I said.

"Looks like apple strudel to me," he replied. He was right.

"Hmmmm," Dad said pointing to the television between bites, "John McLaughlin."

There was a man on the television named John McLaughlin who was being interviewed.

"That was my Father's brother's name, John McLaughlin," he said.

I was confused, "Wouldn't your Father's brother's last name be McShane?" I questioned.

"It was," he explained, "but he joined the English army and went AWOL. He changed his name and ran off to Cuba. They never found him. He just disappeared."

"Did Grandpa ever see him again?"

"Oh yeah, he occasionally came over to the States but not much."

His attention quickly turned from that story as a woman's image flashed on the screen. "That's Ann Richards' daughter. You know Ann Richards, the former Governor of Texas, who said, 'You can't blame poor George Bush, he was born with a silver foot in his mouth.'" Dad started laughing, he always loved that line.

The talk of a Democratic Governor quickly had his mind churning, "How's Hillary doing?" he asked. "I haven't been following everything with the races with all that's been going on."

Dad always had a tremendous amount of admiration for Hillary Clinton. He saw her as a fighter and a champion of those that did not have a powerful voice of their own. It was one of those topics we did not discuss very much. He said numerous times that the last time he was this excited to vote for a presidential candidate was when he cast his ballot for John Kennedy.

"She's crushing Trump in the national polls." Much like with the Red Sox on the first day of the visit, I lied. She was leading Trump in early polling but only by a slim margin and was actually still battling it out with Bernie Sanders for the nomination, although she had a pretty clear path. If Dad was to pass soon, I wanted him to go being excited at having a big winner.

"The analysts are saying she should win by 20 or more points," I continued. "Not going to be a contest."

He nodded, "Good, good."

I laughed months later when Mom said to me on the phone, that it was strange that Dad always talked about how Hillary was crushing Trump in the head-to-head polling.

"Yeah," I responded, "I might know where he got those insights."

Chapter 62

Mom and Dad always had very defined roles. Dad was the provider, the story teller and the person who would infuse you with his passions. Dad would always make sure we were standing up for ourselves and not backing down to challenges outside of our home.

Mom was the comforter and the protector. She would forgive and correct situations that we may have caused or played a hand in creating. Any toughness we exhibited outside on the street with friends or neighbors was washed away within the confines of our home.

Mom was the consummate caregiver. She would silently glide throughout the house, constantly cleaning and cooking without a complaint or a hint of exasperation at the waves of laundry or dishes.

When Marsha was young she had a friend sleepover and at about 8:30 in the morning the friend woke her and said she had to go to the bathroom but didn't remember where it was. Marsha got up and took her to the bathroom, then Marsha walked down the hall to the other bathroom. By the time the two of them got back to the room the beds were made, their clothes were folded and Mom had already begun making their breakfast. They informed Mom that meal time was still a long way away. They each returned to Marsha's room, crawled back into bed and did not re-emerge until three hours later.

I don't think any female ever married into the family without saying the words, "I hope you don't think there is going to be a continuation of the way you were raised."

After a long day on the oil truck, Dad would come home, eat dinner while discussing the day, and then head downstairs to sit in his favorite chair and watch TV until he would drift off to sleep. He had done his job for the day; he earned money and made sure no needs went unmet.

Mom's shift went 24/7. When dinner finished she sat at the kitchen table with us as we did our homework. She reviewed, corrected, quizzed us and challenged us on the level of work we were completing. Most of the time she remained seated quizzing us as we would sprawl out on the linoleum floor of the kitchen providing her subpar answers because our preparation was not very thorough (or not at all in some situations).

As reverberations from Dad's snoring echoed from downstairs, we would be heading off to our bedrooms to turn in for the night. Mom was just getting started. She would be placing a book and a banana on her bedside for late night reading. At this point in the evening, Mom would protect us from anything and everything that our imaginations conjured up in the night. This included the pile of clothes that turned into a ghoul or the Willie Talk ventriloquist dummy that, quite possibly, could come to life as soon as no adults were around to see it happening.

On nights when Dad did not fall asleep and made his way up to the bedroom to sleep for the night, Mom and I worked out a signal to assure me that she was awake. As a young child, it was a fear of mine that everyone would go to sleep before me. I hated to hear the theme music to The Tonight Show with Johnny Carson on the television because it drove home my inability to get to sleep and how late it had become. On these nights I would clear my throat and, after a short while, Mom would clear her throat. When I heard her it reassured me that I was not going at the evening hours alone while also protecting my manhood against letting Dad know I was scared of the dark.

On nights when I would drift off to sleep, if I was awoken by a bad dream (usually a witch, I never liked witches), Mom was the one whose silhouette appeared in the doorway, illuminated by the hall light. She would reassure, comfort and then go back to her room, ready to cough until I was, once again, asleep.

Mom not only protected from paranormal attackers in the night but she also tirelessly protected all aspects of our childhood.

In November of 1978, I was 11 years old and rummaging through the closet in a small room under the kitchen. It was one of those short closets that ran the entire length under the staircase. As I searched for whatever it was I was looking for, I noticed at the far end wrapped presents. I pulled some objects out and dug, and dug to this treasure trove of gifts.

I heard Mom upstairs in the kitchen cleaning but she had no idea that I was exploring this little, space. As I pulled a few of the presents out I saw what my friends had all been telling me but that I had no desire in believing. "To: Patrick, From: Santa; To: Maura, From: Santa..."

It was the proof that I needed but did not want. I trudged up the back staircase into the kitchen and said, "Mom, I just found something out but don't worry I promise I won't tell Maura (she was eight)."

Mom looked at me with a great deal of confusion in her eyes and said, "What?"

I had already questioned her on this and she had rebuffed me on more than one occasion but now she was dead-to-rights. "I was just in the downstairs closet and I saw the presents and I read that they are from Santa."

She sighed and looked down. The pain she was experiencing and showing was not an act. She looked out the kitchen window for a moment and turned back and faced me. "You got me," she said. "Thank you for not telling Maura."

I nodded. Most of me did not want to know the facts. Magic is so much better.

But then she continued, seriously but also as a matter of fact, "If you think about it, there is no way that he can deliver all of them in one night."

"What?" I asked.

"The presents," she said. Nodding like I should fully understand what she was talking about. My confused expression begged her to continue.

"There is no way Santa can deliver presents to every boy and girl in the world in one night, right?"

I nodded.

"He delivers them throughout the year and it's up to the parents to put them out on Christmas Eve, after the kids go to bed. Thank you for not telling Maura."

She turned back towards the stove and started working the frying pan asking me if I wanted a hamburger for lunch. I did. And it all made sense.

And she had maintained a believer.

Chapter 63

Dad had no issue finishing his dessert. Mom walked in the room at that moment and said, "How's he eating?"

"Good," I said.

She looked at the plate, "Doesn't look like such a great job to me," she said.

"Well, he ate his potatoes," I replied, "and his strudel."

"We know he'll eat the sweets. No issue with those," Mom said. I glanced over her left shoulder at the clock. It was 12:20. I had to leave in an hour and forty minutes.

I showed Dad some pictures of my family on my iPhone. He liked the pictures. He loved the phone. "Florence," he said, "look at these."

"I know, Gerard," she said, "but we're not getting an iPad, that's what it's called, right?"

"There are iPads but this is an iPhone," I said.

"It's better than those albums you have," Dad said.

"I'll put a stop to this," she said laughing. Mom turned to me and said, "How much does it cost to have one of those phones with the internet and everything?"

I said, "I don't know, about $400 a year."

"$400 a year?" Dad said.

"Yes," I answered.

"Forget it," he said.

Mom smiled.

The lady across the hall from Dad's room would constantly call for whatever nurse's aide was on duty. There wasn't anything wrong, she just wanted constant attention. Today, the nurse's aide's name was, Estella. So from across the hall, you would hear, "Estella, Estella, Estella, Estella…"

Mom laughed. Dad looked up and said, "What are you laughing at?"

"She sounds like she's in Death of a Salesman," Mom said laughing harder.

Dad started to laugh and said, "Stella, Stella, Stella."

Mom repeated after him, "Stella, Stella."

Mom saw my eyes drifting over to the clock which now read 1:35.

"Gerard," she said, "you know Patrick has to fly home today."

"Yes," he said.

"Do you have to get going now?" Mom asked.

"Not now," I said, "pretty soon, though. 2:00 o'clock."

I had twenty minutes and was working overtime to try and convince myself that I would see Dad again. Now was my opportunity to share my innermost feelings, ask the questions that I didn't know the answers to, delve deep into the psyche of who my father was and what made him tick. I looked at him sitting in that wheelchair and asked the only question that popped into my head.

"You saw Babe Ruth play, didn't you?"

"When I was ten years old," he said. "He was with the Boston Braves. He was all done but it was still something to see him on that field."

Dad sipped his water and continued, "I was in a supermarket recently wearing my Red Sox cap and someone said to me who do you think the second best Red Sox player of all-time is? Everyone knows Williams is the best. I thought for a while and said, Babe Ruth. He just stopped and said that he had never thought of Ruth. He said, you know, you're right."

At that moment, it all became easier for me. I realized that end-of-life is just like life. The conversations are the same. There doesn't need to be a singular, watershed moment that pulls it all together. Maybe it's best to just continue what has always been, especially if what has always been is very good.

"Well, if Williams is the best for baseball, who are the best for the other big three sports in Boston?" I asked.

"Football is Brady, Hockey is Orr," he said immediately, "basketball is tough, either Russell or Bird." He spent some time mulling it over and then shook his head and said, "It has to be Russell, 11 Championships in 13 years. It has to be Russell." He paused and then said, "Does any other city have four players that can match Williams, Brady, Orr and Russell? I highly doubt it."

"Good question," I said. "We'd have to come up with cities that have been around for a while that have all four sports, like Chicago. They could put up Ernie Banks, Walter Payton, Bobby Hull and Michael Jordan."

"I'll give them Jordan but we take the other three," he said.

"How about Los Angeles? They could say Sandy Koufax, Jack Youngblood…I guess would be the best Los Angeles player ever…Wayne Gretzky and Magic Johnson…or Wilt Chamberlain."

"I'll take Boston," he said.

"New York? They could put up Ruth, Lawrence Taylor, Bernard King and Mark Messier."

"Boston," he said.

"I agree. We win," I said.

The clock now read a few minutes past 2:00. Mom glanced back and said, "Oh, you have to go. You have a plane to catch."

Here it was. This was the moment. And I didn't even really think about it, I just quickly stuck out my hand. He raised his hand and lightly clasped mine in a shake. "Bye, Dad, I have to head to the airport," I said, my voice not wavering in the least.

He nodded and said, "Okay."

"I plan on coming back in a couple of months," I said. "I want to fly in to Naples and visit Mike and Marsha and then do the second half of the trip here."

He said, "Good, that's good."

I stood and turned and gave Mom a hug and kiss good-bye. She was so light it was like hugging a shadow.

"I'll call you soon to see how everything is going," I said.

"Okay," she said smiling. "Have a good flight and thanks for coming down. You guys being here made the biggest change in him," she said.

"Thanks. Bye."

I stepped into the hallway and heard Mom start talking to Dad about his lunch. I paused and turned back. Mom noticed me and started to straighten up from helping Dad get a Kleenex.

Dad sat in his wheelchair with CNN playing on the television. The brim of his Red Sox cap blocked me from seeing his eyes. I could see his nose, his right cheek, his mouth and jaw. He tilted his head up at me and gave a small grin.

I raised my left arm and forced a grin to my face.

He raised his right arm a bit and gave a slight wave back.

I softly said, "Bye."

Epilogue

That was the last time I saw Dad alive. He lived another three months and passed away on August 17, peacefully in his sleep. Two of the months he was in good health and working with physical therapy, but then his body began rapidly failing. He was taken off skilled care and put on hospice.

Initially, though, his turnaround was amazing. Having so many of the kids around him with vibrant conversation and humor was like putting jumper cables on a battery. All of a sudden there was a spark of energy and a desire to be an active participant in life. It was someone willing end-of-life to hold off for a while because they weren't quite done.

A few days after I went home, Dad sat with Jim, each reading a section of the newspaper. At one point he opened the obituary section and said, "Hey, will you look at that."

Jim looked over and said, "What is it?"

He casually pointed at the paper and deadpanned, "There I am."

Steve went home about a week after I did and Jim followed shortly thereafter. After Jim returned home, Dad turned to Mom and said, "You know, I think a couple of them thought I was on the way out."

Dad continued to get outside to enjoy the fresh air and to see the activity. Mom and Dad would sit on the front porch of the skilled nursing facility and watch residents and visitors come and go. Mom smiled at him on one of these occasions and said how much she enjoyed these times. Dad's response was succinct, "So that's what our life has come to, huh? Our highlight is watching strangers walk in and out of that door."

I didn't get to call my Dad on Father's Day. Theresa and the kids took me to Fenway Park to see the Red Sox beat the Mariners. It was too loud and there was no way he would have been able to hear me. I texted Maura to relay the message that I said Happy Father's Day and sent a picture from Fenway. Maura replied that he said that it was great that I was there. I tried calling later when we were in the car headed home but Maura had already left the skilled nursing facility.

I did speak with him one last time a couple of weeks later. It was June 27, 2016, his 91st birthday. I stepped outside of my office onto a side street. The bright sunshine beat down as I made my way into the shade of a tree. A gentle breeze lightly shook the branches.

I called Steve's cell phone; he and Jim had gone back down to visit Dad. Steve passed Dad the phone and I wished him a happy birthday. We spoke of the Red Sox and the weather. It was nice. It was normal.

Dad always hated talking on the phone. This was no exception. After five or six minutes he said, "I have to get going."

I held back the laughter and said, "Okay."

Steve came back on the line and I busted out laughing. "He has to get going," I repeated. "Where's he going?"

"I think he might have to use the bathroom," Steve said. "You want a call back when we get him situated again?"

"No, thanks," I said. Dad gets far more pleasure speaking with people who are in the room with him. "Just enjoy your visit." I could tell that Dad had his fill of the phone.

I hung up and stopped and gazed into the parking lot. Everything seemed so still, so peaceful, so ordinary. But I had a feeling that conversation might have been the last time I ever spoke to my Dad. And it was.

While there were many warning signs, I never made it back down to Florida to see him. And I have absolutely no regrets. I had targeted the weekend of September 10 to visit again if he was still hanging on but he was gone. My last visions of him were at his best in a challenging situation. He was conversant, funny and telling stories.

There was a constant flow of siblings so he was never alone. All eight kids were able to get to him at one point or another to have their final moments. Some convinced themselves that what they were witnessing was a challenging situation that could be overcome; others convinced themselves that this was the end of road. It's all part of how we cope with impossible situations.

Four years earlier, when Mom and Dad were 87, he looked at her over breakfast one morning and said that he could not imagine life without her and that he often thought that if she were to die, he hoped that he would go the same day.

Without missing a beat, Mom responded, "Well, if you go first my goal is to stay around for a good, long while so don't get any crazy murder / suicide thoughts in your head."

Now the jokes had subsided and the reality was imminent. By the time he had reached the final 48 hours we were all in regular contact with Mom and Maura. They were continuously by his side and sending each of us updates every hour. His faculties were shutting down.

He ceased responding to any interaction in his last 24 hours, however, the doctors did say that he could hear and understand what was being said. Maura texted that if anyone wanted to speak with him we could call and she would put the phone next to his ear or we could send her a text and she would read it to him.

I didn't call – I couldn't. I sprawled out across the bed in my dark bedroom and racked my brain trying to come up with what should be the final message I ever sent to my Dad. "Thank you" was not enough. "I love you" was not how we communicated.

I rolled onto my stomach still staring at the empty text box. I thought back on our lifetime of conversations. What could I send that would mean something to both of us. For a moment I considered sending him an update on the Red Sox, very casual and conversational. Not a good-bye, just a continuation.

My thoughts turned to his other passions: politics, poker, Mom's beef stew. Nothing was resonating.

Then it struck me: his favorite movie, Gunga Din. At the conclusion of the movie the soldiers realized that they received the adulation while Gunga Din worked tirelessly, bravely and without recognition. They were first hand witnesses to Gunga Din giving everything he had, including his life, for the betterment of others.

At this point, I cried as I typed the final message that would ever be given to Dad from me. It was the same words that the soldiers said over the dead body of Gunga Din.

You're a better man than I am.

The Eulogy That Wasn't

While I was honored to be asked to eulogize Dad at his funeral, I struggled mightily with what to write to show the proper level of respect, humor and celebration of a remarkable life. Reams of paper were used and discarded while sitting in front of the keyboard. A frustration in my abilities was becoming all-consuming and I knew I needed help. I also realized that there was only one person I thought could help. And that was Dad.

Through a lifetime of conversations, I was confident that he could still provide me with all the answers for which I so desperately searched. I sat back in the maroon captain's chair I had pulled up in front of the family computer, closed my eyes and pictured myself back on Country Drive, sitting in Mom's seat in the kitchen with Dad sitting down at the other end of the table, reading The Boston Globe. I pictured how I thought a conversation would go if he was helping me work my way through the eulogy.

The "conversation" with my Dad flowed easily. No surprise. I began furiously typing the notes of our talk. What I came up with was what I was planning to use for the eulogy, until I changed my mind a few days before the service.

In some strange way, even though he was gone, I really felt his presence in this conversation. So here is, "the last conversation."

I visualized The Boston Globe dropping as he looked down the table at me over the top of his glasses.

"What are you doing?" he asked.

"You don't want to know," I responded.

Long pause.

"I'm writing your eulogy."

His eyebrows rose as he gently placed the still open paper on the table in front of him. "I'm gone?"

I nodded.

He took his glasses off and leaned back in his chair. "Huh, I guess I didn't want to know."

He glanced out of the bay window and looked across the street into the Fitzgerald's yard.

"What are you thinking?" I asked.

"That I shouldn't have saved that last piece of pie for later."

I gave a small laugh.

His eyes turned back down the table to me, "Everyone doing okay?"

"As good as can be expected."

He nodded as he looked down at the piles of paper in front of me covered with scribbles.

"There doesn't have to be a eulogy. Just have the Priest say a prayer."

"There will be a eulogy."

He gave a half shake of his head. "Keep it short, give people a break, they've got lives to lead."

"I want to talk about McShane Oil. How you worked for your Dad when you were little and when you came back from World War II you actually bought out half of the business at the age of 19. How you grew the business then ended up buying out your father when he wanted to retire. How you took on a partner in the 1950s because of the growth. I also want to just touch on how you sold the business in 1977 because you didn't want your kids going into that line of work."

"It was a good career but too tough, everyone turned out for the better not being caught up in that life. But, okay, that's all fine."

"Can I talk about you being a Marine?"

"There's nothing to say."

"You joined at the age of 17 and were sent to the Pacific Islands where you were struck by shrapnel while in battle and you had to spend a full year in hospitals before returning home."

"So did a lot of other guys. A lot of them didn't make it home. I served like everyone else. There's nothing to say."

"You crossed enemy lines under fire to save a man and carried him over your shoulder back to safety against direct orders from a superior officer."

"How do you know that?"

"Mom told me."

"She talks too much. Anyone would have done that."

"Other people were there and they didn't."

"Those people put themselves on the line as much as I ever did. There's nothing to say about my time in World War II."

"Can I talk about Mom?"

"Why, it's my eulogy?" He laughed.

"Yes, you can talk about your Mother. Just say how we started dating very young and it worked out great. She was the one who ran the house, she had the tough job, I just had to make money."

He looked down for a moment then glanced up and said, "Oh, make sure you get in there that she is three weeks older than me."

"I will. Anything else?"

"I'm glad I went first."

"Anything about the kids, grandkids or great-grandchildren?"

"Your Mother and I were very fortunate. Everyone turned out to be very decent people. Honest, good people to be around. And the grandkids, how did they end up to be so intelligent? I really have been amazed."

There was a period of silence. The situation overcomes you at times.

I said what I could not find the nerve to say when I was with him last. "I never really said good-bye to you."

"You didn't know I was dying."

"Oh yes I did, but I was too chicken to say good-bye."

"What did you say?"

"I said, 'I'll see you again.'"

He nodded, "Well, that's also the truth."

I returned his nod and grinned. "Any words of wisdom?"

"Only buy something if you've got the money in the bank to pay for it. I don't understand how people can just continuously run themselves into debt."

"Noted. Anything else?"

"I don't know, just, look out for each other. If someone needs help, help them and don't wave your arms looking for congratulations for doing it."

"How should I end this, Dad? Maybe I could try to do one of your signature looks of squinting, slowly shaking your head while looking down and giving an exasperated, half-laugh – you know the "I can't believe you are my offspring" reaction whenever we did something really dumb. Or maybe paraphrase Gunga Din and say, 'You're a better man than I am, Gerard McShane.'"

He smiled, "How about the end of The Last Hurrah?"

Perfect, where Governor Skeffington is lying in bed with family and friends surrounding him and his eyes gently close and they all cry and lament his passing. Right up until the Brahmin political boss says that maybe now that he is standing in front of Saint Peter at the Pearly Gates, maybe now that he is forced to look back upon the errors of his past he must truly repent and if he had it to do all over again, he would surely live a very different life.

And at that moment, when everyone thought he was gone, Skeffington's eyes fluttered open; he looked at the political boss and said, "Like hell I would."

"You wouldn't change a thing, Dad?"

"No, everything turned out really well. I couldn't ask for anything more."

"Do you think I have enough?"

"You have enough."

He picked the paper up from the kitchen table and disappeared behind the large pages.

I sat for a moment and saw his hands holding the sides of the paper and managed a soft whisper, "Okay, I'll see you again."